Guarding the Channels of the Supernatural
by Kim Haney

Cover design by Kim Haney

All Scripture quotations are from the King James Version of the Holy Bible, unless otherwise stated.

Guarding the Channels of the Supernatural
by Kim Haney
Published by Women of the Spirit Ministries
Stockton, California
First printing
Copyright © September 2013
Second printing April 2014
Third printing August 2015

Printed in the United States of America

ISBN 978-0-578-13061-3

Contact author at kimhaney7@yahoo.com

Special Thanks

I want to send a heart felt thanks to those who have made this book possible. One of God's greatest gifts to mankind is friendships and I am deeply blessed to be surrounded by those who I can honestly call friends.

To my best friend in the entire world, Pastor Nathaniel Haney, who I love with all my heart. I'm so thankful for a pastor who believes, teaches and lives a true life of holiness. This walk has cost him valued relationships, but his commitment has influenced countless others including me. I love you.

My dear friend, Regina Lopez. What a gift God has given you to be able to scavenger through my rough manuscripts and make them readable and proper. Above all your talents, I am so thankful for your influence as a godly woman. I love and appreciate you.

My friend, Alana Escalante. You were so kind to help edit this book in it's first phase. As a public school teacher, you have allowed your light of holiness to shine brightly to hundreds of students.

My beautiful mother, Jimmie Beavers. She taught me by her example how a true Christian should live. Mom, you showed me the beauty of holiness.

I give honor to all the beautiful, Christian ladies who have reflected God's holiness in this world. Those who have stood the test and kept their eyes on Jesus instead of being swayed by the pressures of those who have walked away. I thank you for not bowing.

Most of all, Jesus, without YOU this book would not exist. I want You to know that loving and serving You is not a burden.

Table of Contents

Dear Reader,

Within each generation there arises a voice which carries within it's hearing the ring of Biblical depth and power. Kim Haney possesses such a voice and is heard among us in this hour. Her writing herein is an extension of that voice through ink flow, touching powerfully not only the paper upon which it rests, but upon the souls of her readers.

Guarding the Channels of the Supernatural is the result of that touching and now it rests upon you as your eyes drink in and your mind absorbs the depth and power of Biblical holiness truth! Herein is a wealth of explanation, revelation, and insight into the holiness of God and His Word from a woman's vantage point, beautifully written and caressed with prayer to become your personal revelatory possession. To you, I highly recommend this insightful manuscript born out of the author's burden and personal concern for you and yours!

It is my honor to personally know Kim Haney – She is an anointed vessel in the hand of God in this hour influencing our women world wide. May you be blessed as you read from these pages with truth, revelation, and insight I pray. May the anointing in every word come upon you to live, teach, and preach the holiness concepts and understandings penned herein.

In His Royal Service,
Lee Stoneking

Kim Haney, my beautiful and talented daughter-in-law, mother of five beautiful children, wife of Pastor Nathaniel Haney, and First Lady of Christian Life Center in Stockton, California.

One day while in prayer, felt the nudging of the Holy Spirit to begin to write this book. You are now reading the results in **Guarding the Channels of the Supernatural.** As a ministers wife for 23 years she has experienced many things.

Kim writes from her heart about an age-old subject: HOLINESS! She uses stories, Scriptures, sound doctrine and personal experiences to enlighten her readers to the importance of inner and outward holiness unto the Lord.

Through the pages of this book she is very transparent, open, and real. She has shared things that make her vulnerable, but will help other women in this generation who have battled with holiness issues to understand the **whys** and **hows** of this subject.

The book is not only informative, but it is interesting! From the very start she grabs the reader's attention by relating an incident that occurred in the life of me and my husband.

You can feel her passion for this subject as she leads you into the pathway of holiness, for it is a way of life chosen by those who choose to follow God's Biblical plan.

-Joy Haney

The first day I heard the deceiving voice of the thief was in math class when I was twelve years old. I was a preacher's kid. I had never cut my hair, wore make-up, jewelry, or gone to a dance. A voice began to speak to me, "Your hair is ugly" as I began to look at all the girls around me who had very short hair and bangs. For the next two-and-a-half years the same voice tempted, troubled, and tormented me over my Apostolic distinctions regarding my outward appearance.

I became an official card-carrying member of the *fence riding Christians*, as I had one leg in the world and one leg in the church. I was miserable at school because I did not fit in. I was miserable at church because I lived lukewarm in a church filled with Christians who were on fire for God. Finally, when I was fourteen years old, I decided to talk to God about my misery.

It was at an altar during a Tennessee youth camp that I buried my face in the sawdust and I selfishly told God that I wanted to *feel* better. In my youthful ignorance I prayed, "Lord, if You can take this stuff out of my heart..." I did not know what to say because I didn't even know my own problem, but the Holy Ghost did! For the first time in my life the Holy Ghost prayed through me as I said, "Lord, if You can take this *love of the world* out of my heart, I will serve You."

I didn't realize that I had just signed a permission slip for the greatest heart surgeon to do a surgical procedure on my heart. After two hours of heartfelt repentance and floods of tears, Jesus removed the root of the love of the world out of my heart! That was 48 years ago and never again has the spirit of the world deceived me!

Today, an ancient spirit with a brand new label has come against the church of God with tsunami-like devastation. After listening to young, Apostolic women question the biblical doctrine of separation from the world, my heart has been broken and deeply concerned over this younger generation. In deep desperation and brokenness before the Lord, God gave me a vision and extremely heavy burden. In April of 2012, I preached this message entitled, *Guarding the Treasure of His Presence.*

Six months after I preached that message, I was in Stockton, California, at Christian Life Center's annual Ladies' Advance. I was amazed to hear sister Kim Haney's message the first night, *Guarding the Channels of the Supernatural.* She and I had not communicated what the Lord had been speaking to us individually. Oh, how expressly the Holy Ghost is speaking to His Bride!

How I thank the Lord for a young lady like Kim Haney who spoke with such a burden, passion, anointing, and authority! The treasure that satan is seeking to steal is the **manifest presence of the Lord** in our midst. The Apostle John made it very clear in I John 2:15-17, "Love not the world, neither the things that are in the world. If any man love the world, the love of the Father is not in him. For all that is in the world, the lust of the flesh, and the lust of the eyes, and the pride of life, is not of the Father, but is of the world. And the world passeth away, and the lust thereof: but he that doeth the will of God abideth forever."

Kim Haney has written this book with the same burden and passion that she spoke with last fall at Ladies'Advance. She has a passionate love for God and His Word. Read with your eyes but listen with your heart. In these pages you will hear the heartbeat of Jesus, our heavenly Bridegroom calling His Bride to separate herself from the world and unto Him.

Rev. 19:6-9 tells us of a day soon to come:

> "And I heard as it were the voice of a great multitude, and as the voice of many waters, and as the voice of mighty thunderings, saying, Alleluia; for the Lord God omnipotent reigneth. Let us be glad and rejoice, and give honour to him: for the marriage of the Lamb is come, and **his wife hath made herself**

ready. **And to her was granted that she should be arrayed in fine linen, clean and white: for the fine linen is the righteousness of saints.** And he saith unto me, Write, Blessed are they which are called unto the marriage supper of the Lamb."

- Claudette Walker

Introduction

It was summer of 2013, the only eight full weeks I get *off* out of the year. Even more exciting than that, my kids were in Oklahoma for about four weeks visiting (or being entertained by) my parents. Now, if you're a mother, I really don't need to explain to you how having no kids for four weeks is a true vacation in itself. No demands. No dishes. No laundry. No whistle blowing. No cooking for an army. Knowing they would be home soon really made me want to be reclusive, enjoy the quiet, and get some projects done. But it kept nagging…you know…that voice that doesn't say a word but screams louder than a train whistle.

Okay, Lord, I promise You I will start this book in September when reality returns, and I am forced to become disciplined again. But then the Lord reminded me of the girl. He reminded me of how I had nothing to give her.

The beautiful young lady had just graduated from our local university and came to me with questions regarding holiness separation. The questions she presented that day were not addressed in attack mode, but in sincerity and true desire to understand. I sat down with her and went through a couple of scriptures hoping that would suffice to answer all her questions, and gave her a big hug as she walked out of my office. I remember the lump in my throat and the heavy-hearted feeling I felt as she walked out, wishing I had something to place in her hand that would go into more detail on the power that's connected with holiness.

Little did I know that she presently had other voices in her life that were speaking much louder than mine as she slipped through the cracks and into the gutter of deception a few months later.

Today, that young lady who was raised on a church pew, is so far from God and so clouded with religious confusion. I must admit, the feeling of guilt has followed me all these years. I should have done more, I should have been more consistent, and I should have reached further.

Out of this heaviness and determination to help detour another casualty has been birthed this book. I can say with tears in my eyes that I don't want to witness another victim of spiritual destruction!

I have four girls and one boy and I want each one of them to fully understand and embrace this call of holiness so the voice of spiritual fraud can never be entertained or laid on the bargaining table in their lives.

I have read several books on the subject of holiness, and I thank God and the authors for every one of them. They each have ministered to me in various ways and given direction for what God desires, but I have noticed the majority of them are written by men. They are scripturally sound, doctrinally based, and heavily researched, but one thing is missing: emotional connection.

How can a man know how a woman feels inside when she chooses this path of separation unto God? How can a guy grasp the pounding pull of a mall window filled with gorgeous jewelry or the lure of the makeup counter at Nordstrom's? How can they know the struggles that go unseen and often unheard inside the corridors of a woman's mind who struggles with fixing her long hair every morning?

If you are human (and honest), these struggles are there. For some reason God has chosen *us women* to display His holiness to this world. What an honor it is, but it does cost something. Without a doubt, the returns are far greater than the costs.

The message of this book is to awaken us to this priceless possession of holiness that God has given to us. It is more than just a set of rules. It is more than just modest living. It goes deeper than a church tradition or even godly standards.

It is powerful, and it is priceless! It is the elevator that takes you from the first floor of the spirit realm to God's penthouse. Holiness is the gateway or channel for God's supernatural power to flow through His people and into the veins of His church. That's why satan works overtime to destroy and devalue it.

God has ordained pastors and teachers in our lives to teach and establish the lines of holiness in our local churches. It is my desire for this book to be a support to the ministry and to assist in their efforts to build fences and establish guidelines that keep us safe from the predators of the world that desire to steal this wonderful gift.

Under the leading of the Holy Ghost, my prayer is for God to open our understanding to the power of a God-separated life, to bring revelation to this precious walk of holiness, and for us to recognize it for what it truly is.

To embrace it, cherish it, defend it, value it, fight for it, and to live under the umbrella of power and spiritual authority in which God intended His daughters to walk.

Precious woman of God who carries the mark of holiness, you are worthy of double honor.

- Kim Haney

I dedicate the passions that flow from the fountains of my heart into the pages of this book to my four beautiful and godly daughters:
Mychail, Kailah, Giahna, and Aunalee

May you forever embrace the power of holiness.

One
The Pursuit of Possessions

It looked as if someone had moved. The walls where the beautiful, tasseled tapestries and gold-framed pictures once hung now revealed cold, white walls that stood silent with the shame and bitter scars of intrusion. There was an eerie silence that spoke. The leopard patterned couches, the Victorian chairs with their curved legs, the table on which the kids played Monopoly at Christmas time, and the china that had been so carefully handed down through the family generations had now become possessions of a thief.

My husband received the call from the Stockton Police Department that morning. Some of the officers had retrieved documents during a drug bust that contained some of his parents' information on them, and the police wanted to investigate. The documents were not really the main concern of the investigation – it was the woman.

During the drug bust, there she sat. She was propped up at a table, eating instant mashed potatoes out of a styrofoam Kentucky Fried Chicken box – *with a gold fork*. Something was just not right about this picture, so the officers decided to investigate.

As the police traveled down the long, gravel road that day to his parents' home, they had no idea what was awaiting them. When the front door swung open, it revealed the most pitiful sight. Thieves had ransacked every corner of their home. Even the linens had been ripped off the beds, and personal items from the dresser drawers were strewn all over the room in the thieves' attempt to locate money or valuable items. Even my dear father-in-law's safe that housed some family heirlooms, special guns and items handed down from his parents had been removed to the garage and torched open.

God helped my husband's parents recover most of their belongings over time, but I will never forget the eerie feeling that hovered in that house the following months. If you have ever been the victim of a robbery, you know this feeling. When the gold forks were brought out for the next Christmas dinner, we all silently wondered if we got *the one*. All of a sudden the grandkids decided they now wanted mom or dad to accompany them upstairs because being alone wasn't as "cool" as it was before.

If you have ever been the victim of a thief, or have ever had something of value stolen from you, you understand exactly what I'm talking about. I live in Stockton, California, where you are really lucky if you *haven't* been the target of some sort of crime.

Through our neighborhood watch program, I have been shocked and amazed at the bravery of thieves these days! It is not your typical nighttime thieves anymore. These people are cutting wires to alarm systems, drugging people's dogs, and breaking in during broad daylight. They are people who are driven to steal another man's valuables.

Let me tell you something about a thief. He really doesn't care about the underwear in your drawer or your old tennis shoes in which you feed the chickens. He could care less about the awesome skirt you found at the thrift store last week and wouldn't think twice about the box of See's Candy you stash in the top shelf of the kitchen cabinet. All he's after are the **valuable things in your house.**

A thief wants the items that cost you something…the things that would be important and precious to him. Like the wad of money you hide under the left corner of your mattress, or the diamond ring that was handed down from your great grandma that's covered in the back drawer. A thief learns your ways. A smart thief will park across the street from your house and watch you for a couple of weeks to learn your pattern. He knows what time you leave for work each morning, and he knows when your kids get home from school. He takes note of the times your valuable things are not being guarded.

The Bible does not give us too many detailed descriptions of satan, but there is one thing it lets us know about him: **Satan is a thief.**

> The thief cometh not, but for to **steal**, and to kill,
> and to destroy (John 10:10).

Satan's methods and techniques of approach are to steal. Just like the creeps and thugs that roam the streets of our cities, satan's methods of approach are sticky, slimy, sneaky, sly, tricky, deceitful, and unfortunately, many times clever.

A thief is effective in his mission because he's deceptive, and the hardest enemy to fight against is the one who knows you the best. As carriers of truth and children of God who display the holiness of

God through our lifestyle, satan doesn't desire to steal just anything from you and me.

This may shock you, but sometimes we give way too much credit to the devil. Satan does not care about our finances, our joy, our job promotions, or our ministry as much as we think he does. We are living in the last days, and our Lord Jesus is at the door ready to call His bride home!

Even though our enemy does not know the day or the hour, he senses the times and seasons and knows his time is short. This is a desperate hour for the thief and his eyes are aimed at the church of God's priceless possessions! He wants the possessions of value – powerful, spiritual value. Material items can be restored, rebought, rebuilt and repaired, but once something of spiritual value is stolen, it can never be replaced.

Two
God Chooses the Channels

It was about two years ago, I was actually in the bathroom getting ready for bed, when out of the blue these words spoke clearly into my head, "Study the Nazarite vow, study the Nazarite vow." Well, I had read the story of Samson many times and had a basic understanding of what the Nazarite vow involved, but I knew there was something God was desiring to show me. I'll have to admit, I'm not really a person who enjoys studying. I hate to read. I would rather be busy doing something. So, it's not like I jumped at the first opportunity to dig into studying the Nazarite vow. Just being honest.

One morning, about a week after this had happened, I awakened early for my prayer time, and I felt the Lord remind me to look at the Nazarite vow. (I'm so glad He is persistent with us stubborn ones), so I opened my Bible and began to read. If you have ever had a true, supernatural revelation take place in your life then you know what I'm talking about when I say the words of that Bible became alive. Right there in the floor of my closet, I had such a powerful encounter with the presence of God as I began to weep over this understanding He was giving me regarding Samson's vow. I knew I was not smart enough, educated enough, or studious enough to understand this on my own, but there was a purpose for this revelation - a heavenly purpose that was greater than I had realized at the time. In my feeble attempt, I want to share this with you.

When we think of Samson, we automatically think of Delilah and the methods she used to get the secrets to his supernatural power and great strength that had been given to him by God.

I want you to walk with me into the life of a young Samson, his days before Delilah. He reminds me of many of our Pentecostal young men today. In Judges 13 it gives us some insight on how Samson was raised in a godly home with parents who were ultra dedicated to the service of Yahweh. He was born a Jew and raised in a very conservative Jewish home.

Samson was the son of Manoah, whose wife had been barren. Have you ever noticed how God sometimes caused barren women to bear the child through whom He would work? This was done as a sign of God's involvement with the child from the start, and any glory of accomplishment was to go to God. It brought added respect to the chosen servant, which could help him accomplish the task God gave him to do. Samson was taught the truth of the one true God just like all the other Jewish boys; however, Samson had something in his life that was very valuable. It was something the others did not have. He was chosen by God and hand selected for a special anointing to rest upon his life.

I don't know why God chose to give you and me this beautiful revelation of truth. I know I don't deserve it nor did I do anything to earn it. This revelation of the one true God and being able to feel His presence the way I do is the most precious treasure attainable to man. I guess that's why it's called the *pearl of great price*, as the Bible likens a person who is willing to sell everything they have to buy it. Bottom line: We have the treasure for which this world is searching.

To be able to fellowship with the presence of God in the way that we do, to feel the divine touch of the Master's hand upon our lives, to have a refuge, a fortress, to experience the power and demonstration of God Himself manifesting in our midst is worth more than any amount of money.

As this world gets darker and more evil, the gift of His presence is becoming more precious to His people. Whether you know it or not, we possess something others do not. Every Sunday in church we have many visitors from various beliefs that do not embrace or understand this revelation, and the comments are always the same, "I've never felt anything like this before. I could not stop crying. There is nothing like this."

Is it because you and I are more spiritual? Is it because we have a nice building filled with friendly people? No. It is the power that takes place when you connect the apostle's doctrine with holiness. You cannot have one without the other because it won't work. Like the cold air meeting the hot air, when the two connect it causes a powerful surge of lightning and electricity. Doctrine and holiness go hand in hand to 'create' the power we encounter.

Samson was chosen by God to walk in this same type of anointing and power.

The angel of the Lord paid a visit to Samson's mother before he was born and told her there were specific things that must be avoided and abstained from in order for this special anointing to remain upon Sampson's life;

> For, lo, thou shalt conceive and bear a son; and no razor shall come upon his head: for the child shall be a Nazarite unto God from the womb: and he shall begin to deliver Israel out of the hand of the Philistines (Judges 13:5).

God always requires commitments when He chooses someone. I don't know why, but He does. The presence of the Lord is precious and the power of God will only operate through vessels that are obedient, separated, and willing to abstain from what He asks. Remember this - *God chose* the channels of separation that Samson was required to apply to his life in order for this supernatural power of God to flow through him.

Samson was required to live by God's stipulations and to abstain from things in which others were not required. That's not always easy. There were hundreds of other Jewish young men during this time, yet something divided Samson from the others. Was he smarter than the rest? Was he more dedicated to the Torah? Did he pray longer and harder than the others? It was none of these, but it was his commitment as a Nazarite; doctrine and separation walking hand in hand.

The thief took notice of his valuables.

The word "Nazarite" means to *consecrate through separation*. When a person took the Nazarite vow, it was a leap beyond the traditional commitment of being a Jew. This type of devotion was not some *private, internal, undisclosed, personal, secret closet-commitment to God.* The Nazarite did not take this vow of commitment because he was born a Jew and raised to worship Yahweh. Honoring religious tradition was not enough, nor did "religion" have the strength or power to keep him committed. This vow of consecration was displayed through external or outward marks of distinction to where everyone around knew who he was, what he was, and Whom he served.

I want to stop right here. We have to really fall in love with Jesus, not just church. There are so many among us who love *the church*, the fellowship of the church, the church meetings, and the culture of the church, but they never really fall in love with the God of the church. These are the people who struggle. They are always questioning and riding the fence line. They never sell out to God or grasp the deep embedded value of the power of separation. They become like Esau with his birthright and become willing to sell their most valuable possession for something that temporarily satisfies the flesh, all because they are void of a relationship.

All five of my children have been raised in this precious truth, but I fear for them. I fear the possibility of them becoming so caught up with the culture and fellowship of the church as it becomes so entwined into their lifestyle, that they could easily never realize the value of holiness and separation, and much worse, never really know God.

Holding on to traditions, passing on the family legacy, and protecting your roots and lineage are important, but they will not keep you committed. It's not only you and me, but it's my kids and your kids who are at stake in this generation. The voices that are speaking into their lives are too loud and consistent for them to hold to traditions alone. The influences that have access to them through the blatant, unashamed world of social media and the scheming, devious voices of the internet world pull at them day by day, hour by hour. So many have become victims through entertaining hidden and concealed deadly voices that speak wickedly and craftily through the window of a computer or cell phone.

I don't ever want this precious path of holiness to become just a leadership or platform requirement, a church standard, or even just a lifestyle of modesty to them. If they ever underestimate or fail to realize the value of the power of holiness, it will take them to a place of apathy where they will no longer guard or protect one of the most valuable possessions given to them by God. This is where the thief will enter. To really understand the value of this God-required separation from the world, you have to be so in love with Jesus Christ and truly know Him. When you walk with Him, out of that relationship comes a deep desire to please Him.

God gave this mother a wake-up call several years ago regarding the importance of my children knowing *Him*. Every morning before school I get my kids up about fifteen minutes early, have a small devotion, and then send them to their rooms to pray. It's not always easy doing this, nor is it always convenient. It never fails that someone is in a bad mood or didn't get enough sleep … okay, you know what I mean.

Occasionally I catch them off guard and ask them, "Do you know why I do this? It's not really because I enjoy it. It's not because I don't have anything else to do. I do this because I want you to know God for yourself. I want you to learn how to pray and how to communicate and fall in love with Jesus yourselves!" Many times I have told them that when I see one of them becoming cold in their souls, or starting to become weakened toward the things of the world, I ask God to send heartache or trials into their lives. I know that sounds really cruel, and they don't like it when I say that, but I know without the heartaches I have personally had to face in life I would never know Jesus like I do now.

I have watched each one of my teenagers take their turn on the Potter's wheel, but during these times I have heard them crying out to God in the privacy of their room. Like the little lamb who is being lured and pulled outside of the sheepfold not really understanding the danger that lurks in the darkness, the gentle, loving shepherd breaks one of its little legs and keeps it close to his heart and close to his voice. Once the leg heals, that little lamb learns to love the shepherd and stays close to his voice and away from danger.

I said all that to say this: Religion alone will not save us nor does it have the power to keep us abiding by certain "rules." Sold-out commitment comes from a deep yearning to know God and to please Him - His way. This can only be birthed through developing a relationship with God and as parents it is our responsibility to plug our children into God, which comes from teaching them how to form a prayer life. Only a consistent prayer life has the power to keep them connected and possessing a hunger for God. Once you have experienced the power, freedom, and blessing that comes with a surrendered heart, you never desire to look back toward Sodom.

If religion and culture alone did not have the power to hold to this type of devotion in a Nazarite, what drove them to this consecrated lifestyle? The men and women who chose to take on this sacred vow to their God knew that the deep things of the Spirit, the response of the supernatural, only came through one doorway.

The door God chose was through certain and specific *outward displays of commitment* that were selected by God. In other words, separation through holiness.

> Nevertheless the foundation of God standeth sure, having this seal, the Lord knoweth them that are his, and let everyone that nameth the name of Christ depart from iniquity (II Timothy 2:19).

The vow-takers did not get to choose what these commitments would be. They didn't wake up one day and decide they were going to cut McDonald's french fries out of their diet, abstain from social media, or give up their favorite cappuccino for a month in order to tap into the realm of the Spirit. No, these were things that were specified by GOD alone. He had to choose what these commitments would be in order to take them to this level of the supernatural, and **they didn't always make sense.** But honestly, has God ever made sense to our human reasoning? I will have so many questions for God when I get to heaven, but until then it's not my place to question Him; it's my duty to obey and please Him.

Numbers 6:1-8 tells us what was required by God to become a Nazarite:

> And the Lord spake unto Moses, saying, Speak unto the children of Israel, and say unto them, When either man or woman shall separate themselves to vow a vow of a Nazarite, to separate themselves unto

the Lord:

He shall separate himself from wine and strong drink, and shall drink no vinegar of wine, or vinegar of strong drink, neither shall he drink any liquor of grapes, nor eat moist grapes, or dried.

All the days of his separation shall he eat nothing that is made of the vine tree, from the kernels even to the husk.

All the days of the vow of his separation there shall no razor come upon his head: until the days be fulfilled, in the which he separateth himself unto the Lord, he shall be holy, and shall let the locks of the hair of his head grow.

All the days that he separateth himself unto the Lord he shall come at no dead body.

He shall not make himself unclean for his father, or for his mother, for his brother, or for his sister, when they die: because the consecration of his God is upon his head.

All the days of his separation he is holy unto the Lord.

Right here, in verse 8, it tells me that in *God's perspective* separation is holiness! We hear people say, "Well, it's just good disciplines, or modesty, or a religious dress code." God specified that the act of separation is considered *holy* in His eyes. Look at verse one with me again:

> And the Lord spake unto Moses, saying, Speak unto the children of Israel, and say unto them, When either man or woman shall separate themselves to vow a vow of a Nazarite, to separate themselves **unto the Lord.**

Notice when they would partake in these acts of separation, they were actually separating themselves UNTO the Lord. Not just separating *from something*, but actually attaching themselves *to God* through these certain details in which God required them to abstain. I don't know about you, but that is empowering to me.

God said, "If you want the power of My Spirit to rest upon you in this dimension, there are three outward displays of commitment that I require of you."

What did God require?

> 1) They were not to drink wine or eat grapes of any kind including raisins.
> 2) They were to let their hair grow. It could not be cut in any manner.
> 3) They were never to touch anything dead or come in contact with any type of corpse – even if a sibling or parent died.

I don't know about you, but none of these three things God required make any sense to me. Why wouldn't God want a man to cut his hair? I can picture a Nazarite looking something like these guys who walk around town with long dreadlocks or with a long braid down the middle of their backs. To human thinking this really does not make a lot of sense. There is absolutely nothing you can point to and say, "Wow, I see and understand why God didn't want them to cut their hair." I cannot tell you why there was some deep, spiritual connection to this commitment God required.

I don't understand why they were not permitted to touch a corpse when everyone else around them was allowed to do so. What if someone they loved passed away and they were secluded from the family when it came time for the burial? What if one of their children died? Maybe it was for sanitary reasons, but to connect this with something spiritual does not make any sense.

What logic does it make to abstain from grapes? Now wine and strong drink I can understand a little better, but grapes and raisins? To look at it from a nutritional standpoint, they are good for your body. They are full of vitamins and minerals that keep a person strong and balanced. Human logic says to eat them.

My friend, the bottom line is this: God's ways do not always make sense! The things God requires of us do not always add up to human logic and are not always the easiest things to do. For instance, in II Samuel 18, it made perfect sense for David, as a leader over thousands, to number the people and to set captains over them, but God said not to do it.

Through the ages, every generation has had an opportunity to question God's requests and decisions in their mind and then make the choice whether or not to obey.

You can search the Scriptures throughout the life of Samson, and you will find God never disclosed *why* He chose those certain outward signs of dedication. God never went into detail about the scientific methods or theological reasoning of *why* Samson could not eat grapes or cut his hair.

We look for the *whys* too often and in our searching we miss out on some of the greatest spiritual formations and blessings that could possibly take place in a person's life. We will never understand God's ways. God blesses and moves through the channels of obedience, not through logic and understanding. When we understand this and learn to embrace what God calls holy, it will lift us into a realm of the Spirit that can come through no other method. There is power in obedience, but there is spiritual strength and authority in obeying when it does not make sense. There is a supernatural power that is connected to these commitments God requires!

I want to share with you a testimony given by Nancy, a friend of mine:

> Although I was raised in church most of my life, my parents were not completely sold out to God, and my hair was always cut, as was my mother's. As I reached adulthood, I continued to cut my hair and didn't think much about it because I never understood the reasoning or power behind it. I surrounded myself with friends who called themselves *Christians* but never lived a separated lifestyle, and I was no different.
>
> As a young woman I experienced several heart-breaking situations that were brought on by the law of sowing and

reaping until I got to the point where I felt like my life was spinning out of control with no real purpose or direction. I found myself praying, crying out, and pleading to the Lord to help me. I was so desperate for a real change, a real relationship with God, and I knew in order to receive this it required commitment. I was tired of living life with no true commitment because living on the fence is miserable!

I finally asked myself, "Do you believe the Word of God? Do you think your church is teaching truth?" It was time for me to make a decision: I was either going to live in or out of church. I knew without a doubt my pastor and my church was preaching the truth, but it was up to me to obey it. I came to a place in my life where I was so hungry for Jesus and tired of my unstable lifestyle I chose to give everything I was to God, including my hair.

I was so desperate for a closer walk with God. That is when he helped me realize that through complete surrender and trust in Him and His Word, there was so much more for my life. When I began obeying the Word of God and stopped making excuses for my flesh and pride, my life changed in such a way that I know now can only come through complete submission to the Word of God.

I had married a man who was not a Christian at the time and didn't understand the lifestyle of holiness and separation, and the enemy kept telling me that my husband wouldn't find me attractive anymore and that he would probably leave me for someone who had cut hair. However, as my hair started to grow out, it was so opposite of what the enemy told me. One day I even heard my husband proudly telling his co-workers that his wife didn't cut her hair and noticed him becoming more possessive toward me.

When my old friends came around and started asking me why I stopped cutting my hair, I would answer, "When you love someone you want to please them, and I love the Lord!" He gave me 14 verses in His Word about the power of a woman's uncut hair and how it matters to God.

Now, my life's purpose has become so clear to me. I have two daughters that have been influenced and affected by the decision I made years ago, and I wouldn't trade that for anything in the world. The life of total surrender to God took me to a spiritual realm that is so close to Him and His presence; it's a place I was never able to attain before I gave Him everything. I now have peace and joy in my heart no matter what life throws at me. He gives me the power to be an overcomer through the spirit of holiness.

How did these mysterious methods work that God had chosen? These strange requests that didn't make any sense and without any explanation, how did they work in Samson's life? They worked as a conduit or a channel from which the supernatural power of God flowed.

And the thief knew it.

Three
Sources of the Supernatural

Over and over the thief watched Samson. He studied him; he took note of the things he desired and the things he despised. He noticed the friends he hung out with, the food he liked, and the people he hated. The thief quietly watched Samson's every move and took special interest in his weaknesses because there was something extremely valuable Samson possessed.

The thief was not after Samson's heritage. It wasn't his doctrine. It wasn't his belief in Yahweh or Jewish customs. He did not attack Samson's prominent position as a judge in the community or touch his bank account. None of those things were touched. None of those items were attacked first in Samson's life because satan was after *the source*. He targeted his attacks on Samson's most valuable possession – the source of his power with God.

A thief usually does not steal everything at once. A thief searches for the most valuable things first, then will return for the other possessions at a later time.

Growing up my husband had a very dear friend. This young man had a very rich anointing upon his life and the Spirit of God rested upon him in a special way. They would pray long hours together, go on extended fasts, study the Word of God, and share spiritual experiences – things you can only share with those who understand.

One day they were chatting in an office and out of the blue his friend turned to him and said, "Nathaniel, I don't believe that standards (or outward displays of our commitment to God) have anything to do with holiness. I believe they are just good disciplines."

My husband knew that day the enemy was after his friend's soul. He tried to reach for him several times. They would sit down and go over the Scriptures, but he chose to believe the lie that separation was not important. What was sad was this young man had sat on the pews of Christian Life Center most of his life.

He had witnessed incredible miracles and had watched people get out of wheelchairs and walk. This young man had been in services where the Shekinah glory of God filled the sanctuary with a hazy, gray smoke as people fell prostrate on the floor under the power of God. The miraculous was no stranger in his life, but he did not value the channels through which God chose to move. They became devalued and somewhere along the way he listened to the wrong voice that brought questions, questions demanding to be answered with logic as the thief worked his way into his life.

To this day that man lives completely blinded by the enemy, and everything of spiritual value has been stolen from him. There is no longer a strong doctrinal belief, and he will baptize you in any name under heaven that you desire. Their services are void of anointing as they have become like any other church. He doesn't even believe it's necessary to speak in tongues to receive the Holy Ghost! It all started with an attack on holiness – not doctrine.

Listen to me friend, satan knows how powerful these channels of holiness are to God's people and he will bring all kinds of voices into your life in order to rob you of your most valuable possession – the power and anointing of God.

Holiness is God's key to the supernatural! It is the channel or the pipeline that the anointing and power of God flows from into our lives, into our families, and into our churches. There have been numerous times we have had visiting ministers from other denominations that do not understand or embrace holiness walk into our Pentecostal services. They have proclaimed through tears they have never felt anything like it. They have expressed to my husband they want what we have.

The thief knows this secret.

He knew this was Samson's secret. Satan knew Samson's power was directly connected to the things from which God required him to abstain. If he could sneak in the back door of Samson's life and steal the conduit to the source of his power then the presence of God would eventually be lifted and cut off from his life. That would only be the beginning. Once the presence and power of God is void in a person's life, everything else will eventually follow.

It would be like getting access to the key to the front door of your home. Once a thief had the key to your front door, he wouldn't have to sneak around to the back or look for an open window. There would be no reason to wait until the sun went down to gain entrance into your house if he had the key. If the key were stolen first, then the thief would have full access to your most valued and treasured possessions; nothing would be hidden and nothing would be safe.

Once satan is able to steal the pipeline from which the power flows, things you never dreamed you would walk away from or would reject will become worthless. Samson's separation was his key to the doorway of the supernatural and power with God! These things were not just a set of rules or religious duty.

Even Jesus Himself, who was God manifest in the flesh, had to have the power that was connected with holiness. When He walked on this earth as a man, the Bible declares this special anointing and power that rested upon Him came from the spirit of holiness.

> Concerning his Son Jesus Christ our Lord, which was made of the seed of David according to the flesh; And declared *to be* the Son of God **with power, according to the spirit of holiness,** by the resurrection from the dead (Romans 1:3,4).

This certain power did not come from deity. It did not come from prayer and fasting. This power came specifically from the spirit that is birthed through holiness.

I feel the need to sound an alarm to someone reading this book right now. Take notice of what and who is speaking into your life. Many times these voices come through good meaning "friends." The Word of God should be the loudest voice in your life right now and forever. Nothing in this world is worth losing your connection with the anointing because you possess what this world is seeking and satan knows it.

The thief will send voices into your life telling you that nothing will change and all will remain the same if you let some things go … just like he told Samson. Do not give a listening ear to anyone who would despise or speak against the laws of God!

> Do not give that which is holy (the sacred thing) to
> the dogs, and do not throw your pearls before hogs,
> lest they trample upon them with their feet and turn
> and tear you in pieces. (Matthew 7:6). AMP

Holiness empowers us to operate in the realm of the Spirit like nothing else; it works as the conduit for God's power to flow through to break the powers of hell and evil. As you continue to read the pages of this book, I pray God brings understanding and revelation as we dig into more detail, and that a fresh appreciation and love for the ways of God would be renewed and strengthened inside each of us.

Four
What is Holiness?

In June of 2013, my husband and I took our five children to Israel for about ten days. If you have never been to the Middle East, it's hard to describe the feeling of the Middle Eastern culture. People of every age, profession, gender, and color, who are absolutely consumed by their religion and the gods they serve surround you. There is not much "middle of the road" in Israel, and I'm not referring only to the Jewish people. Everywhere you go, every restaurant, shop, or street corner, every face you pass unashamedly proclaims the god they serve. Not with their voices, not with signs or bumper stickers on their cars, not with fliers or religious tracks, but through their bold outward appearance.

My girls and I walked the crowded alleys of their Arab markets and passed shop after shop of the Muslim women's "modest" clothing that would put our Christian clothing to shame. From the top of their heads to the soles of their feet, they are covered in thick, dark-colored, coat-like clothing – even in 100-degree heat.

We can walk into our local Wal-Mart and come face to face with a pair of eyes staring through a black veil that covers the entire face of the woman behind it. If you compare apples to apples when speaking of separation or modesty, the extreme Muslim women would make

Christians look like heathens. There is one thing that vividly sticks out to me: their god is shown and unashamedly displayed by their follower's strict dress codes.

Does this mean those who dress modestly but follow false religion and worship false gods are considered holy? If not, what exactly is holiness?

Holiness is not only separating *from something*, but it's separating unto God Himself. To be separated *from,* without being *attached to* God is nothing more than just being different. When we are unified with God, the entire process of separating from the world unto God is now defined as being holy. It is God who makes our acts of separation something holy because we are attaching to the only One who is completely holy.

> And one cried to another and said, Holy, holy, holy is the Lord of hosts; the whole earth is full of His glory! (Isaiah 6:3)

> There is no one holy like the LORD, Indeed, there is no one besides Thee, nor is there any rock like our God. (1 Samuel 2:2)

There is no other god who is truly "holy." The Lord Jesus Christ is the only God that a human can attach themselves unto, and it be considered holiness. My husband and pastor, Nathaniel Haney, explains it this way:

> Your Bible is the most precious possession you will ever own. When all else fails, the precious Word of God will not fail.

The Bible is made up of two testaments: The Old Testament and the New Testament. The Old Testament contains the writings and covenant that was in effect before the cross. The New Testament contains the new covenant writings because of the cross (or after the cross). This book supplies us with all we need to understand who Jesus was, how to get close to Him, what pleases Him, and what displeases Him and how to understand His nature. God opens our understanding to His Word so we can know Him.

Pastor Haney further states how the Word in the Old Testament describes the Lord.

For I *am* the LORD your God: ye shall therefore sanctify yourselves, and ye shall be holy; for I *am* holy: neither shall ye defile yourselves with any manner of creeping thing that creepeth upon the earth. For I *am* the LORD that bringeth you up out of the land of Egypt, to be your God: ye shall therefore be holy, for I *am* holy. (Leviticus 11:44-45)

Notice here, God was referring to a person being holy as being separated from certain things that He detailed and specified in the preceding verses. The reason they were to be holy (or separated) was because they served a holy God.

There is none holy as the LORD: for *there is* none beside thee: neither *is there* any rock like our God (I Samuel 2:2).

Hannah proclaimed there was not another god who was holy besides the Eternal God, or the God of the Holy Scriptures.

Exalt the LORD our God, and worship at his holy hill; for the LORD our God is holy (Psalm 99:9).

David voiced throughout the Psalms that the God of Israel was a holy God.

> To whom then will ye liken me, or shall I be equal? saith the Holy One (Isaiah 40:25).

There are literally hundreds of Scriptures throughout the Old Testament who proclaim God as being holy. Through the books of the law, the historical books, the poetic books, and the prophets all teach that God is holy.

Pastor Haney further explains that when the New Testament came along; God did NOT lose His holiness!

> The cross of Calvary did not erase the fact that our God was still holy. Some people believe that since we are living in the Dispensation (or time period) of Grace, we now have the freedom to live unrighteously or however we desire. But the New Testament teachings are consistent with the Old Testament teachings in that God is still holy and His people are to live holy.

> And now I am no more in the world, but these are in the world, and I come to thee. Holy Father, keep through thine own name those whom thou hast given me, that they may be one, as we *are* (John 17:11).

As the humanity of Jesus was speaking to the Spirit, He describes the Father as being "holy." If God is our Father and we are His children, we must inherit the DNA of His holiness. The children must desire to be like their Father.

> As obedient children, not fashioning yourselves according to the former lusts in your ignorance: But as he which hath called you is holy, so be ye holy in all manner of conversation; Because it is written, **Be ye holy; for I am holy** (I Peter 1:14-16).

Here Pastor Haney shows us the necessity of God's people to be holy and separated unto him both in the Old and New Testaments. I thank God for a pastor who still preaches and teaches the power of holiness!

The word "conversation" in this verse means "lifestyle" which encompasses our words, our actions, thoughts, and dress. Again, holiness is referred to as lifestyle. You have to remember, the world does not understand this. They see the way we dress and regard it to be a set of rules and a code of strict religious conduct, and they question why. There is *no way* for them to understand the calling to be holy because they are children of the world.

The god of this world is their father and his spirit, which is the spirit of disobedience, is working in them. This spirit will never allow them to understand or experience the power that is associated with a child of God who carries the mantle of holiness.

The world, especially the religious world, despises the fact that we are a people who live consumed inside and outside by the God we serve. The god of this world hates distinction and "absolutes" as evident in the fashion world today.

Satan has been working for years to blend the genders and create a unisex society. There are spirits associated with much of today's clothing, especially clothing stores out of Europe.
When you understand prophecy, you see through that veil of material and see the spirit of antichrist that is working in our world today, and I must add, very strongly.

You can Google topics on holiness and get a real eye-opening picture of how the world – especially those who have walked away from the holiness of God- despise and attack it. We will discuss why later. They even have entire websites and discussion panels that debate holiness and separation from the world – like they can literally vote, comment, and debate against God! Someday God will laugh at them.

The world will never be able to comprehend the ways of God, first of all, because it's none of their business. They are reading someone else's mail. God wasn't even talking to them - they are reading what God wrote to the church! The Holy Scriptures were never addressed to them, and the Spirit that wrote the Bible does not even live inside of them. The god of this world blinds them, and it is impossible for the children of the world to understand anything about holiness unless God gives them a revelation.

But I thought holiness was only a heart issue?

> For the wrath of God is revealed from heaven against all ungodliness and unrighteousness of men, who hold the truth in unrighteousness; Because that

which may be known of God is **manifest in them**; for God hath shewed *it* unto them. For the **invisible things of him from the creation of the world are clearly seen**, being understood by the things that are made, *even* his eternal power and Godhead; so that they are without excuse (Romans 1:18-20).

It is an obvious thing that no one can see someone's heart. I cannot see your heart, and you cannot see my heart. The heart is a spiritual object that cannot be seen by human eyes or touched with human hands. Only God can actually see and know someone's heart.

According to Romans 1:19, the things that God knows and sees about my heart will eventually be made manifest (or outwardly shown and displayed) through my life and lifestyle. Did the Apostle Paul say these things were sometimes seen? Inwardly seen? Barely seen? No. They are *clearly* seen. This business of "My heart is holy inside and God knows my heart" many times comes from those who do not desire to obey the scriptures.

It is true that some people have never properly been taught and are often repeating the words of the voices around them, never really realizing what they are saying. Yes, God does know your heart. He also knows it's in rebellion against His Word when you're not living according to what He desires. Everything about us mirrors Him. Even other religions know this secret.

My husband and I were ministering at a church not long ago, and a lady I was talking with told me the story of how God used her power of holiness as a witness. She worked at a large bank branch and had worked her way up to a high level of position as a financial consultant. There was a middle-aged man who had recently inherited a huge sum of money. She had consulted with him previously, but he had not made any firm commitments. Every consultant in that branch secretly reached for that man's business and one day he walked in to make some investments.

This Christian woman happened to be off work that day and another woman greeted him, eager for his business. He looked at her and said, "I want to talk with the Christian lady." The other woman explained that she was off work that day and added, "Well, I'm a Christian too." The fact was, she did not *look* like a Christian, and this man knew it. He looked at her and said, "No, I want to do business with the lady who *looks* like a Christian." Now, this guy was by no means any type of Christian, but he knew the mark of a true woman of God! It was how God was demonstrated through her first on the inside followed by the outside.

As someone once said, "Live in such a way that those who know you but don't know God will come to know God because they know you." People in this world cannot see God, they cannot see someone's heart, but they can see the visible identification that a man or woman of God portrays in the way they look, talk, dress and act. It's our duty to allow the God inside of our heart to be made manifest so the world can see what it means to truly live for Jesus. The Lord Jesus doesn't walk the sidewalks of our cities anymore. The only way God can now become visible is through you and me. Wow!

This is another reason the thief wants what we have.

I cannot tell you the countless times my daughters and I have walked into a store or restaurant and, without ever saying a word, a complete stranger makes a statement about God, faith, or church. My daughter Kailah and I were shopping in a thrift store not long ago and a nice older gentleman started a conversation with us over some item in the store. I had noticed he noticed us when we entered. I had never mentioned one word regarding us being Christians, that we attended Christian Life Center, nor did I offer any type of witnessing tract. Before that conversation was over, he was saying things like, "The Lord bless you, have a blessed day, etc." Our witness was in the way we were dressed! He knew us by our outward fruits that accompanied a kind, warm, and caring conversation.

Let me say right here: the Holy Ghost anointing follows you wherever you go when you walk in the spirit of holiness! I have literally felt the presence of God walk into a store with me many times and felt His Spirit flooding the aisle where I was standing. People who were in close proximity felt it, too.

Outward holiness is one of the most powerful witnessing tools you will ever possess, and the thief knows it. It tells everyone around you who and what you are. It reveals Whom you serve, and opens doors to those who are hungry .

In March of 2014, my husband hosted a prophecy tour to the land of Israel. On a visit to Qumran, we had a few minutes to shop as approximately one-hundred Pentecostals, with their skirts and long hair, flooded the store. I was in a corner looking at some soaps when one of the employees, a young, jewish woman, approached me. She motioned me over the corner, and in her broken English asked who we were. I began to explain we were from America and Canada, and on a tour of the Holy Land. She stopped me and said, "No. Why are you different? Why do you wear skirts and have long hair?" She continued to explain how she watches thousands of people come through the shop each year (most of them professing Christian groups) but had never seen anyone like us. Sensing a deep and longing hunger in her eyes, I began to explain the reason we are separated from the world is because we serve a holy God. As we stood there in that crowded store, I felt the power of the Holy Ghost reaching for her as tears began to brim her eyes. Our conversation was interrupted by some needy customers, but before I walked away she wrote down my email and wanted to know more about what she felt that day in the store.

Outward holiness separates us from the others. The Holy Ghost is not given to us just for us to have a great experience, but it's given to change our lives. When this inside experience is demonstrated and displayed on the outside, it becomes like a magnet for those who are hungry and searching for God.

You know what I mean, when they start up random conversations because they are not sure of what it is that they are feeling radiating off you. This channel of anointing is powerful when you realize what you have hold of! It will go before you when you're facing a tough social situation. You will be the one contacted and called when a friend is in desperate need of prayer.

I feel the Holy Ghost so strong right now as I am writing this. I believe someone is receiving a revelation of the power that is accompanied with holiness! We must embrace this, protect it, and defend the channels of the supernatural God has given to us. I want you to read again how Jesus Himself walked in the supernatural power that was birthed through holiness:

> Concerning his Son Jesus Christ our Lord, which was made of the seed of David according to the flesh; And declared *to be* the Son of God **with power, according to the spirit of holiness,** by the resurrection from the dead (Romans 1:3-4).

> For thou *art* an **holy people** unto the LORD thy God: the LORD thy God hath chosen thee to be a special people unto himself, above all people that *are* upon the face of the earth (Deuteronomy 7:6).

In Hebrew, the word "holiness" is translated "Qadash" or *kaw-dash*. It's definition is to "consecrate, sanctify, dedicate, be separate, to keep ones self apart or separate." Yes, it's very important to be holy in your heart, but to be separate is going to involve some outward dedication as well. The difference between being "sanctified" and "holy" is that *sanctification* is the process of becoming holy. The Greek word translated "sanctification" (*hagiasmos*) means "holiness." To sanctify, therefore, means, "to make holy."

To sanctify someone or something is to set that person or thing apart for the use intended by its designer.

I would like to mention a powerful explanation that Reverend Eli Lopez, senior associate pastor of Christian Life Center, taught recently:

> We all have a starting point in our lives that the Bible calls justification. It's the point where we are regenerated, born again, and made a new creature. It means "to be declared right in the sight of God." It's not based on our good works, or how good we are, but God looks at us as being 'right' in His sight because once the blood of Jesus covers our lives,

God's righteousness covers our lives. Just think about how frustrating this is to satan because he knows about our mistakes, he knows about our faults and failures, but God's blood covers them all.

This is the beginning point in our walk with God. The end is called "glorification" and none of us are there yet because it's the end result of salvation. There is a journey we walk between justification and glorification, right in the middle there is a pathway called "sanctification." Sanctification is the process of living out our justification. Sanctification says God saved me, and now I'm going to live out that salvation on a daily basis. It's a place where we learn how to live a different life and how to *live out* the salvation we received. This is the road we travel on learning how to be a Christian. The closer we get to the end result of glorification, we should become more like Him.

To grow in sanctification is to grow in holiness, for holiness is synonymous with sanctification. The way sanctification is lived out in our lives is through holiness.

In one sense, only God is holy (Isa 6:3). God is separate and distinct, and there is no other. No human being shares the holiness of God's essential nature. There is one God. Yet Scripture speaks about holy things. How does God call human beings to be holy, as He is holy? (Lev 11:44; Matt 5:48 ; 1 Peter 1:15-16). God calls His own to set themselves apart for that which He has chosen.

Now, back to my original question, "Are those who dress modestly but follow false religion and false gods considered holy? If not, what exactly is holiness?"

When a Christian receives the Holy Ghost, there is now something holy living inside of them. As they pray and develop a relationship with God, something begins to change inside as their values, morals, and views of the world change. This is the process of sanctification as we begin to desire to put away worldly things, hunger to become pure, and draw nearer to God. This takes place at a different pace in each person's life, and sometimes those who have lived for God for a number of years must be patient with what God is doing in someone else's life.

I remember several years ago, a woman who attended a charismatic church in another city visited one of our services. Right away she felt the power of God in a way she had never experienced, and she wanted what she felt. We gave her and her two children a bible study on baptism in Jesus' Name. (She had already been filled with the Holy Ghost), and I will never forget what happened.

She went down into the baptism waters wearing bright red fingernail polish. As she came up out of the water, she lifted her hands up to God and as she was lifting her hands she saw the bright red nail polish and jerked her hands back down into the water. She said she could no longer raise her hands to a holy God wearing her bright red nail polish. Nobody had said a word to her about her nail polish, but in her sincerity and her deep desire for God, she felt the convicting power for herself. God gave her revelation of separating herself unto Him.

About a year later this lady and her children were instrumental in starting a Oneness Pentecostal church in her city that is still going strong today! This is not a common story. Most of the time people have to be taught, led by the Holy Ghost, and develop a relationship with God as they go through the stage of sanctification, and we have to be patient and display the Spirit of Christ during this time.

You see, anyone can be separated into a religion. I could convert to Islam and cover myself from head to foot, and be dressed "modestly." I would have adapted a very rigid, disciplined religion in which to be dedicated. I could convert to the new age teachings and dress differently. I could begin tapping into the universal force and allow my life to be controlled through positive thinking. I would still be separated from the majority of the western world. I could take the rigid vows of a nun and live in a convent the rest of my life, dress in Coptic catholic robes, or become a Buddhist monk and shave my head.

These examples are not "holy;" they are only "separate." Separation alone cannot make you and me holy. Anything people separate themselves to outside of God still makes them part of the world's system. It may be different or divided from what the majority of the population does, but it's still not connected to the One True God Who is holy.

Look at the Pharisees in the Bible; they were a people who separated themselves from other Jews and Gentiles, but they did not separate themselves unto God so they never became holy – they just became separate. People's search for God has become more evident than ever before as they are trying these strict religions of the world and not finding what they are seeking.

What I'm trying to convey is that separation in itself does not bring power and anointing. You must be separated unto, or attached *to God,* while detaching from the world. God alone, the One you are attaching yourself unto, is the one who makes you holy.

This is why you must have a relationship with God! Your relationship is what begins this process of true holiness because it starts on the inside (which we will cover later). When a person starts drawing close to the Lord, Who is divinely holy, they will begin to take on His nature, which has no room for legalism. When this happens and you have that unification and connection with your precious Lord Jesus, it's not *your* holiness that is birthed, but it's the nature of the holy God that is living inside of you. This supernatural power takes hold when the Holy Ghost comes into our lives and joins us with God. From there we begin the road to true holiness.

Five
Outside Inside

We live on about four acres of land that consists of horses, sheep, dogs, cats, and occasional rabbits and other begged-for animals. Our property is loaded with some huge, gorgeous oak trees as well as other types of trees. In the back corner behind our garage sits one of the most beautiful, majestic oak trees I have ever seen. It's one of those trees that look "perfect" with its huge, thick branches and deep green foliage. I noticed this tree years ago when we first tried to purchase the property.

Last winter we had a massive rainstorm come through (okay, it was massive in California terms), and in the middle of the night I heard this loud crash take place. As I peered out the window into the dark, I could not see anything so I went back to bed. The next morning I saw it.

There it lay. Its huge majestic limbs detached from its body and lay in a heap like an arm that had been amputated. The limbs that fell weighed hundreds of pounds and smashed my son's basketball hoop and all the fencing that surrounded it.

The amazing thing about it was that there was no possible way for anyone to tell this tree was diseased inside. It had beautiful, green leaves. It looked strong and healthy. There was no outward sign of decay or corrosion, but somehow a disease had attacked and began to work on the inside of this gorgeous tree.

I walked outside one day and just stood and stared at the broken limbs lying there on the ground. As I stood there, I was moved in my heart, and I talked to God saying, "Lord, please don't ever let me become diseased inside." I've been around "diseased" *holy* people. You have, too. Those that look the picture perfect image of what a godly person should be on the outside, but on the inside they are so full of venom they could out strike a rattlesnake. Enough said.

If you have lived long enough, you have, at one time or another been a victim of one of their strikes. We have all heard the expression, "Hurting people hurt people." This is so true. It comes out in the subjects they choose to talk about; it shows forth in the way they treat the waitress at the restaurant, or the guy in the Burger King drive-thru window. Don't get me on this subject. I have been so extremely embarrassed being out to eat with *ministers* who have treated waitresses like they fell off another planet.

My late father-in-law, Reverend Kenneth Haney, was one of the best examples I can possibly think of when I think of a holy heart. During his funeral, there were mentions of his passionate preaching and organizational abilities, but over and over again it was repeated how he treated people with kindness.

Story after story was told, with tears streaming down their face, how Kenneth Haney treated the "little" people. The people whom nobody had time for. I remember him telling me of a book that every couple of years he would take off his shelf and read again. The name of that book was, *How to Win Friends and Influence People* by Dale Carnegie. This could be classified as a very spiritual book, as the subject it addresses is: servanthood, giving to others, humility, taking your eyes off yourself and looking at others, etc. Dale Carnegie states, "A great man is known by the way he treats little people."

I have stopped in my tracks and deeply considered the way I treat people outside of my church and my family. I may be the only Jesus they will ever see. I have lectured my kids more times than I want to admit on the importance of going out of your way to be kind to the outside world. If we look "holy and separated" on the outside, they already know we are Christians without saying a word. How powerful Jesus will be portrayed if our hearts back up our outward witness by speaking love, kindness, taking time to listen, smiling, giving compliments ... you get the picture. Jesus told us the secret of showing forth His love to this world, and I think we miss this sometimes.

> Even so, every good tree bears good fruit, but a bad tree bears bad fruit. A good tree cannot bear bad fruit, nor *can* a bad tree bear good fruit. Every tree that does not bear good fruit is cut down and thrown into the fire. Therefore **by their fruits you will know them** (Matthew 7:17-20).

What a powerful witness we are for Jesus when our inward hearts reflect our outward appearance! These are the times when you can *feel the power* of His anointing flowing through your life to someone else. When the inward and outward become synced together, there is no greater witness on this earth!

What breaks my heart is all the Christians who live in unnecessary, internal bondage. I have traveled many places and have witnessed so many hurting Christians that live in a secret world of pain and internal wounds, wounds that cause and produce so many other spiritual diseases

Believe me, I'm no saint. May I be transparent enough to confess that at one time I have been one of these "diseased" *holy* people? I have walked the path of bitterness and tasted of its fruits, and because of this I am more determined than ever to check my heart. This inside, or internal "heart" holiness is something I have to work on every single day of my life. I repent often and sometimes that is not enough. It's a constant battle between this heart of mine and allowing the nature of Christ to flow, operate, and transform me, because I understand that my outward appearance has no power until my heart is right.

One of the thief's most powerful methods of embezzlement is through offense.

When a painful offense takes place, it goes straight to your heart.

I have a dear friend who has a very powerful testimony. I will call her Angie in order to protect her identity. Angie has gone through some stormy waters and faced some unbelievable situations, but she now understands the power God's healing can bring. It was her desire to share her testimony with you in order to throw a lifeboat out to someone who may be drowning in a sea of pain. Her story offers hope for you today:

> I have had the Holy Ghost for over 25 years. What I have gone through has brought a deep respect for the Word of God and the power and protection it gives when we obey it. In March of 2008, a door opened that started me down a path that would forever change my life.
>
> My husband and I were receiving counsel from one of the pastoral staff members of our church, when under the guidance of the Holy Ghost he suggested I open up regarding the abuse and trauma I experienced as a child. I had never done this before. Reluctantly, I began with my parent's divorce at the age of one. My father was a raging alcoholic, and my mother was emotionally manipulative and controlling.
>
> The sexual abuse started when I was six years old, and at the age of seven I was diagnosed with type-1 diabetes. The abuse did not stop until I was fifteen. When I was twelve, I told my older brother (who was one of three abusers) that our stepfather had taken advantage of me while our mother was in the hospital. My brother hated our stepdad and called Child Protective Services, within 48 hours my stepfather had committed suicide.
>
> I was told by my mother that the incidents were probably my imagination and to never discuss them again. The abuse with my brother continued and he was later convicted of another sexual abuse incident and sent to prison.

I knew I needed a lot of inner and emotional healing as the memories and flashbacks would haunt me in the secret places of my mind. Even though I knew Jesus was walking with me, I came to the place where it seemed I just could not move forward. I cannot express the anger, the bitterness, and the frustration that began to consume me. I became depressed, started having panic attacks, and could not sleep at night. I began to take on the victim mentality, as I felt entitled to my pain and anger. My faith began to waver, and I felt like a hideous person, disgusting inside and out, as the enemy began to attack my mind with thoughts that these things that happened to me defined who I really was.

In the midst of all my pain, the thief slipped right by my side. I stopped going to church regularly, and when I did go I began to question everything the pastor said. My bitterness was taking me down a dead end road, but I was so blinded by my pain I could not see it.

It was in early 2012 when I received a call from my younger brother asking me if our mother could move back to California where she could have help when she needed it. My mother was not attending church and had been diagnosed with borderline personality disorder and bi-polar disorder. I actually felt validated for the first time in my life that this was definitely a disease I was fighting and not simply a person. I agreed to have her come live with us just until she could get on her feet.

My husband and I knew there would be some trouble, but we did not grasp the severity of the situation until she got here. There were a lot of things my mom did that brought chaos and pain, but this experience was far worse. In my confused and disoriented world of pain, I asked her to just *trim* my hair. I did not cut my hair, but the wounds in my spirit and the bitterness I carried were causing me to feel so far and separated from God as I began to feed on the lies that I was ugly. I had allowed the influence of my mom and the bitterness and anger I still carried inside to separate me from the presence of God – and I could feel it! I became deaf to the voice of God, and like Samson with his head lying in Delilah's lap, I was totally ignorant of what the enemy was robbing me of as she began to cut my hair.

Half way through I began to smell alcohol on her breath and noticed her hands were trembling so I stopped her immediately. It was then that I realized *how much* of my beautiful, God-committed hair had been cut off. I ran to my bedroom closet, shut the door, and bawled.

The shame I felt was beyond words, how could I have let her do this? My crying woke up my 13-year-old daughter as she came to check to see if I was all right. How was I going to explain this to her? As I opened the door, my face red and swollen, I looked her in the eye and said, "Mam cut my hair." I was so ashamed I could not say anything else. She hugged me and said, "Mom, it will grow back," and she was right, but there was a much deeper violation that took place that I could not explain. I felt like a piece of me had been cut off along with my hair. My soul felt so heavy because I knew my supernatural covering had been lifted.

It's hard to describe the depth of emotions that took hold of me that day, as the shame and regret became overwhelming. I can look back now and see how the thief came in when I was broken and unguarded. He took advantage of my injured spirit as he walked right into the doorway of my life and stole something of great value, a channel of holiness, which allowed me to become more vulnerable to the attacks to come.

The anger turned to deep depression as things began to really spiral downward in my life. I began to lose sight of the important things like my husband, my children, and my relationship with God. I began entertaining thoughts of suicide. That's exactly what the thief's objective is: to first steal, then to kill and destroy, and I was on that path to destruction.

My mother moved out of our home, and immediately we could tell a difference. Things were getting back to normal, but I was still struggling. I only went to church once or twice a month and would come up with excuses why I wasn't there. The truth was I didn't want to be there. I didn't want to be around people as the distorted thinking that accompanies depression clouded my mind.

One day my pastor's wife, Kim Haney, contacted me and wanted to meet for lunch so we could talk. We talked over two hours that day, we laughed and cried, and I began to talk about the things I had been dealing with the last few months. I could feel Jesus reaching through her to me as she said, "Angie, you are a miracle! You have come too far to give up now." I drove home with tears in my eyes, knowing that something took place in my spirit during our talk. I was thanking Jesus for what He was doing, and I made up my mind I would go back to church on Sunday.

As I walked back into the sanctuary that Sunday morning, I couldn't tell you how relieved I was to feel His presence again. Something had changed in me that day at lunch, and I didn't realize to what extent. God had begun a healing process in my life that is still in effect today.

I went to the altar with such desperation to touch Jesus and His presence was so real to me that day. I cried and prayed so hard that I felt I was trembling under the power of this God who loved me so much. I began to cry out to God asking, "Jesus, what do I need to do? I cannot leave here the same way I came. I need help now!" He spoke so clearly, "You need to let go of everything you have held onto over the years. You have allowed the wounds to act as a protective wall around you; now it's time to let it go. Don't hold anything back because I paid for this, and it doesn't belong to you!"

I saw myself opening the door to my wounded soul, pulling these things out one by one, and handing them to Jesus. I had to come face-to-face with all the hurt, the disappointment, the anger and the bitterness. As I cried out to God, "Lord, take these things and anything else that would hinder me from being close to You," a complete miracle happened. I was instantly delivered from depression, as if a cancer fell off me. There, at that one moment in time, a deep healing took place, and I knew I would never be the same.

I have never felt so free in all my life! Every morning I get up excited to spend time with Jesus. The Lord has walked with me as I traveled this long road of healing.

The first thing the thief attacked in my life was my separation of holiness. In my desperate attempt to make myself beautiful and attractive I allowed my hair to be cut, but it only made me feel worse about myself.

I can see now by allowing the channels of God's power to be cut off in my life (like when my hair was cut), it pushed back the protective covering of God and allowed the power of the enemy to settle over my life. This thing is real, and it's powerful! No matter what I face in life, I know that Jesus is with me, and He has placed principles in His Word that when obeyed, provide protection for my family and myself. Nothing in this world is worth losing that covering! I will forever guard and protect the presence of God in my life and home.

Your heart is the central operating system of your entire being. It may be unseen, but if the heart gets corrupted, so goes the man or woman. I have watched solid, Christian couples get offended or hurt by someone in the church, and instead of going to them and making it right or seeking forgiveness, they allow that wound to bleed and get infected. The next thing you know that couple is ready to leave their church that teaches sound doctrine and attend some congregation that is filled with deceptive spiritual lies.

I have personally watched couples in the church go through literal hell in their lives. From their kids getting strung out on drugs, losing jobs and barely being able to put food on the table, fighting with incurable diseases that have brought pain and suffering, to dealing with major attacks in their marriages. Things that rip your heart into pieces. Secretly inside I have wondered if some would ever make it through their trials without throwing in the towel and giving up on God. Much to my surprise I have watched these people fall upon the Rock, become broken and empty before God in the midst of their storm, and come out different people. I watched how their physical trial actually brought them closer and more dependent upon God as they made it through these horrific storms.

I have also watched in amazement these same people become *offended* by someone in the church, and the next thing you know the Pastor has a letter of leave on his desk. These same people, who have weathered major storms in their lives, made it through some of life's most troubling battles, are now ready to leave the church and walk away from truth due to the effects of an offense.

Beware of the schemes of offense! Sometimes we are blinded to its power and purpose because its not a physical attack, but an *internal attack* and involves feelings and emotions. Attacks upon the heart can be more deadly than physical attacks!

Have you ever noticed how bitter people are drawn to congregations that have walked away and detest outward holiness? Again, we see the footprints of the thief entering through the open window of offense to gain entrance into our souls.

The thief knows how sacred holiness is.

How do sincere, Christian, Holy Ghost filled people end up living in inner bondage? This process takes place through thought patterns and thinking too much and too often on what a person did or said, as spiritual bondage begins to form inside the corridors of that person's heart. They can look the same, go to the same church, sing in the choir, run the aisles and worship God, and even speak in tongues but inside live in captivity. I understand this because I have been there. If I am speaking to you and you desire help, I encourage you to get my book, *Christians and Strongholds*, which goes into greater detail on healing power.

We have heard people say, "God is the foundation of my life," and there have even been songs written about it, but that is not Scriptural. The foundation of your life is not your prayer life, it's not your faithfulness to God's house, and it's not even your knowledge of the Word of God, although these things contribute to keep your foundation strong.

The foundation of your entire life is built upon the condition of your heart. The Psalmist knew this when he penned:

> For, lo, the wicked bend their bow, they make ready their arrow upon the string, that they may privily (or secretly) shoot at the **upright in heart**. If the foundations be destroyed, what can the righteous do? (Psalm 11:2-3)

"Privily" literally means *in darkness* and this is where the enemy does his work. Secrecy is his greatest weapon, and as long as we allow him to work in the darkness and secrecy of our hearts, light and healing will never come. The thief is not after our health, our finances, our jobs, our children, or our faith as much as he is out to corrupt our hearts!

Satan knows that sin and defilement are things that will separate us from God. He knows first hand when we allow sin into our lives, it causes us to lose the spiritual dominion God has given to us. Satan watched with glee what happened to Adam and Eve.

People don't understand many times that there is a much bigger picture involved than just harboring a little bitterness, jealousy, or pride. It's connected to the power, authority, and dominion God has placed in our lives as His children. Satan hates you because you have replaced what he used to be. You have ownership of something satan and his forces want back, and he will go to every extent to get it.

> And they sung a new song, saying, Thou art worthy to take the book, and to open the seals thereof: for thou wast slain, and hast redeemed us to God by thy blood out of every kindred, and tongue, and people, and nation; **And hast made us unto our God kings and priests**: and we shall reign on the earth (Revelation 5:10).

We have now become sanctuaries unto our God! Satan looks at you and me with a jealous hatred and says, "I used to be that. I used to be a king and have dominion and power." Now he sees God has given you and me that dominion and power!

The thief knows **holiness keeps you connected** with that dominion and power.

How is your heart? Don't just read past this paragraph of the book, really think about it. How are things inside that secret place inside of you? Your heart really does speak to you – sometimes very loudly. My friend, are you dealing internally with pain and bitterness over something someone did or said to you? Does jealousy control how you treat others? Pretending or playing "Christian" allows you to ignore the true condition of your heart. Eventually your heart's condition will come out, and every attempt you make to control it will fail.

The issues that you tolerate or refuse to confront will eventually begin to control your actions, your character, your relationships with others, and eventually take over your personality. Everything must pass through our hearts first to wherever it's going. Everything.

> Keep (or watch over and protect) thy heart with all diligence (it's a constant thing); for out of it are the issues of life (Proverbs 4:23).

The Pharisees thought the outward symbols were more important than the condition of the heart. Jesus came along and plainly identified and revealed the importance of first guarding your heart when He said:

> Blessed are the pure in heart: for they shall see God. (Matthew 5:8).

Those who keep their hearts pure will see God not with the natural eye, but with a special spiritual vision and closeness is the message Jesus was sending. A man or woman who constantly watches over his or her heart will be brought into a special relationship with the Lord that is obtainable no other way.

I cannot end this chapter without offering you hope and a way of escape - God's way. It's the only way that works. Someone reading this book has been wounded and hurt by something you didn't deserve. Someone has felt the bitter, sharp pain of rejection.

I have three close friends whose mothers have rejected them since they were children. I have watched the painful effect this kind of rejection has had upon each one of them, even through their adult years. I offer you hope today because I can offer you the Healer. No matter how hard life's blows have been to you, Jesus not only is able, but He is willing to heal your pain. Remember? This is His job description:

> The Spirit of the Lord God is upon me; because the Lord hath anointed me to preach good tidings unto the meek; **he hath sent me to bind up the brokenhearted, to proclaim liberty to the captives,** and the opening of the prison to them that are bound (Isaiah 61:1).

We live in a home that is about forty-three years old. In our backyard, we have a wooden awning that spans over our patio area to keep it shaded. This has become one of my kids favorite hang out places because half of the wood planks are rotten and fall through to the ground. They gather these up and make things like fishing poles, artillery weapons and swords.

One day, our then nine-year-old girl Giahna, came in crying and holding her finger. She ran over to me and opened her hand; there sat this huge boulder of a splinter lodged deep inside her little finger. She had gotten it from one of those fallen wood pieces. I tried to squeeze it out, but nothing worked. It was so deeply embedded in her finger that I knew we had to resort to the needle.

This is where her dad comes in... Now, I've seen my share of blood in my time, but for some reason I have a hard time sticking a needle into my little kid's finger. Dad takes a look at the splinter and decides surgery is the best approach (his type of surgery involving a needle – him being the surgeon). Instantly, at the sound of the word "needle," we have an instant miracle.

All of a sudden the splinter doesn't hurt anymore. Giahna is now jumping around the room promising it doesn't hurt.

Being the sweet and gentle dad that he is, Nathaniel sits Giahna on his lap and explains to her why this ugly splinter must come out. It can cause major disease or blood poisoning if it's allowed to stay in. Even though she didn't understand everything, she was tired of the pain it was causing so she entrusted herself into the hands of her daddy.

As she sat there on his lap, he took the needle and began to dig out that rotten splinter out of her little baby finger. It hurt. The tears that streamed down her cheeks were evidence of that. Even through the painful experience, Giahna knew her daddy was doing this because he loved her. He plucked that splinter out little by little as the object that was causing her pain was being removed.

Do you have splinters in your life that you have never allowed your heavenly daddy to take out? There are things that have happened to you that you did not deserve. He sees the tears that roll off your cheeks and fall on your pillow at night. He watches how you're hurting and noticed when the splinters began to blister and infection begins. *But you must trust Him enough to allow Him to pull them out.* You have to take them to Him. *You* have to bring them out from hiding and allow them to be vocalized. Sometimes that is the most difficult part of it all.

Can I tell someone reading this book right now: go crawl upon your Daddy's lap and show Him your splinters. Allow that little child inside of you to come to Jesus. You need to cry over some things that have been causing you infection and let God use His needle so you can be healed. I promise you this; He will hold you close to His heart as He takes out the splinters of your life.

I don't know if we can truly love Him the way He wants us to love Him if we never go there with Him. Your wholeness will come as deeply as you allow the healing to go; only then will you truly understand the freedom that comes with being *holy inside.*

Six
Beware of the Voice

After my husband's parents had their home broken into, I remember wondering how in the world the thieves were able to steal so many items. Usually when a break in occurs, you will find only a handful of items missing, but a whole houseful?

The police explained to us that the first initial break in was a "test." The thieves tested to see if there was an alarm system hooked up, if neighbors reported anything unusual, or if there was any type of defense activity taking place. When no signs of protection were signaled, no security alarms went off, and no signals of defense were indicated, they went in for the loot. Apparently, they had literally backed up a U-Haul type truck to the back garage in preparation for all the items they were planning on taking.

The sole purpose of a thief is to steal only valuables. He knows the moment he steps foot inside your home he only has seconds to do his job because someone might wake up and call the police. Or, if you lived in the Haney household, you might find yourself face to face looking down the barrel of a shotgun.

Knowing he may only have one shot at taking something, satan is going to go for the jugular vein of spiritual power in our lives. Please hear me. It's no accident that holiness is almost always the first possession to be stolen. Have you ever noticed this? When someone walks away from this precious truth, it's not with the intention of ever leaving the doctrine, but it's the holiness and separation that becomes the victim of attack.

Satan will test us to see if we will neglect to guard the very sources and channels of God's power in our lives. Once they are gone and the presence of God is cut off, everything else will eventually follow because the borders and boundaries have been removed.

I have had people in my life that I never would have dreamed would someday embrace the doctrine of the trinity or ever allow Jesus Name baptism to become a subject of controversy. It's when they began to allow certain voices, who seemed so innocent, into their lives that caused them to question whether holiness was really essential to salvation, or whether it was something required by God to be saved.

Can I say to someone reading this: be careful of the voice! Take notice of the voices in your life. It's not usually the sinner or the religious world you have to be cautious of, but it's those who have walked away and left this precious truth. Scriptures reveal that these people are working under the operation of the spirit of antichrist:

> Little children, it is the last time: and as ye have heard that antichrist shall come, <u>even now are there many antichrists</u>; whereby we know that it is the last time. They went out from us, but they were not of

us; **for if they had been of us, they would no doubt have continued with us** (in truth): but they went out, that they might be made manifest that they were not all of us (I John 2:18,19).

There is a spirit of antichrist already heavily at work in this world that wants to attack truth of, "the Lord our God is one Lord" and everything for which it stands. It tells you all roads lead to God as it works to attack the work of Calvary and anything that allows the supernatural power of God to flow through His church.

The first method of attack satan has ever used on mankind was his voice. He sends questions or often times sends *people* that tempt us to question God's laws. Beware of the questions. There are some things you just don't discuss with the enemy. When a person gets to the place where they would even lay these sacred truths on the table of discussion, something is wrong. Most of the time it's not the actual question that's involved, but the spirit of the question as we see in Genesis 3:1:

> Now the serpent was more subtile than any beast of the field which the LORD God had made. And he said unto the woman, **Yea, hath God said,** Ye shall not eat of every tree of the garden? (Genesis 3:1)

The first thing satan does in his method of violation is get a person to question the Word of God. Is the Bible without error? Is it absolute? Is it infallible? If he can get us to the place of questioning God's Word and doubting His voice in our lives, then we have no anchor. Notice when satan came to Eve he did not try to deny God or come with any other type of temptation, but he came to her with a question, "Hath God said?"

Voices have so much more access to our world now than even five years ago. Through connections via social media such as Facebook, Twitter, Instagram, and other social sites, there is a new open door into our lives. Social media has taken the world by storm, and there is nothing you and I can do about it but try to protect our kids by setting boundaries. People we would never normally fellowship with now have access to our minds and spirits through posts and comments they make on these social media sites.

No face to face interaction means being free to say anything and free to speak what they would normally never image telling anyone to their face. They feel entitled to say things out loud, and satan uses this device cleverly! Turn people away and delete them from your accounts when there is a voice being streamed through this unseen world that constantly attacks or offends your faith. Be aware of the voices!

Most of the time he sends the questions in the form of people, oftentimes friends. Satan knew the Word of God and was able to take the pure Word of God and twist it into a question that was wrapped in the spirit of deception. We have to recognize what the spirit of hell is up to. It sees you and me as virgin souls who have been washed in the precious blood of Jesus, living a pure and clean life, and it wants to steal this power from us.

The power of the voice is what took Samson down that long road to destruction. It wasn't his involvement with Delilah. It wasn't the scissors that cut at his long locks of hair. The thief took a "test" run in Samson's life way before Delilah ever came on the scene. Satan used an old and time-tested method to gain entrance into Samson's house - his voice.

It was something that has worked for him from the beginning of mankind and still is in operation throughout the ages. When a method of entrance keeps working for a thief, it's the first thing he uses to gain entrance to a new victim.

The VOICE of the enemy began to speak when Samson was alone. "Do you think these ridiculous vows are really important? Look at all the other young Jewish men, they don't have to live so set apart. Your parents are old fashioned. Besides, they are the ones who committed you to this lifestyle; it was not your choice."

Like a broken record, the voice began to play this over and over again in the hallways of Samson's mind. What's so deceitful is we often think we are the ones thinking these thoughts. The thief does not show up looking like a masked bandit wearing a gun and holster; he comes into our lives through the invisible realm and attacks our thought patterns. Then, once he realizes he has gained some ground into our minds, he will send other voices into our lives to confirm what we are thinking or questioning is right.

Samson was on his way to catch a woman. He had chosen a woman out of the Philistine tribe, and as he was on his way to marry her, a lion jumped out at him and started to attack. Judges 14:5,6:

> Then went Samson down, and his father and his mother, to Timnath, and came to the vineyards of Timnath: and, behold, a young lion roared against

him. And the Spirit of the LORD came mightily upon him, and he rent him as he would have rent a kid, and *he had* nothing in his hand: but he told not his father or his mother what he had done.

Take notice friend of mine. When you are going through an attack of the enemy upon your life, when you have absolutely nowhere to turn or anyone to turn to for help, when you're facing satan with nothing in your hand, it's *only the power of God* that will protect you from the attacker. The thief knows this! If Sampson had not been walking in the power that his *separation* brought upon his life, we would be reading the end of his story. When you walk under the umbrella of holiness and live a separated life unto God, you can lay claim to the promise of Isaiah 54:17:

> No weapon formed against you shall prosper, and every tongue *which* rises against you in judgment You shall condemn. **This** *is* **the heritage of the servants of the Lord,** and their righteousness *is* from Me (Isaiah 54:17).

If Samson had only realized what he had! If Samson had only guarded and protected that power and anointing that was upon his life. If he had only realized that through these channels of abstaining from what God had told him, connected with his doctrine, came his power and authority. Instead, he listened to the voice.

It was the voice of compromise, the voice of questioning, the voice of reasoning and logic. The thief knew if he could steal the conduit or the pipeline from which this power flowed, the presence of God would eventually be lifted and cut off from his life.

Notice the subject of attack:

> And after a time he returned to take her, and he
> turned aside to see the carcase of the lion: and,
> behold, *there was* a swarm of bees and honey in the
> carcase of the lion. And he took thereof in his hands,
> and went on eating, and came to his father and
> mother, and he gave them, and they did eat: **but he
> told not them that he had taken the honey out of
> the carcase of the lion** (Judges 14:8,9).

Months later, on that same road, Samson remembered the dead lion
he had killed. The thief had paid Samson a visit many times before,
and he entertained questions of whether this "separation" part of his
commitment really mattered to God.

Apparently, Samson listened to the voice as he walked over to the
dead carcass of the lion. God said, "Don't touch anything dead!" But
inside of that dead lion's carcass was a big hive of honey, and the
battle began. Do I touch it? Does it really matter? Does this illogical
instruction really make a difference, or is it just a tradition? The
voice spoke more loudly than ever before; it always does the first
time around.

The thief stood quietly by and watched the inner torment of two
worlds colliding as the allurement of the honey dangled before him.
Don't do it! No, Samson, don't compromise! Guard this precious
treasure of God's power in your life! Remember this, satan always
uses things that are alluring to our flesh. Our flesh is the hardest
thing to fight. This is another reason he attacks holiness because it
involves the sacrifice of our fleshly desires. In a weak and unguarded

moment something was stolen. Samson didn't even realize it as he reached out for the honey and touched the dead carcass of that lion.

There was no atomic bomb that went off, there was not another lion waiting to destroy him, and God struck no one dead. That would have been too obvious. **The thief knows you don't lose the glory overnight.**

The presence of God did not depart from Samson the first time he let go of something. The Bible does tell us that Samson felt shamed by what he did. Notice how he responded to his parents in verse nine, *"but he told not them that he had taken the honey out of the carcase of the lion."* He didn't want them to know he had touched something dead. This tells me there was a war going on inside Samson's mind. He felt the shame that comes with dishonoring the laws of God.

One of God's greatest gifts to men is the gift of conscience. Have you ever done something and quietly hear God whisper He didn't like that? One of the most dangerous places a Christian could possibly be in is where conviction no longer bothers them.

In I Thessalonians 4:4-5, Paul tells us we will know, through the leading of God's Spirit and direction of the Scriptures, how to walk in the paths of holiness:

> That every one of you should know how to possess his vessel (your vessel refers to your body) in sanctification and honour; Not in the lust of concupiscence, even as the Gentiles which know not God:

This tells us that the world should not define our lifestyle or moral code. We get our moral code from the Word of God. The Scriptures refer to God's Spirit as the "Holy" Spirit for a reason. When we are filled with this Holy Spirit, God will change us and give us a portion of His holy nature which will produce change in our lives.

When you have the Spirit of God inside of you, you will know the voice of God. It is not God's plan to just let us decipher things on our own once we are saved. You will learn to know His voice and the guidance of His Spirit.

> My sheep hear my voice, and I know them, and they
> follow me: (John 10:27)

Notice how God did not withdraw His presence from Samson the first time he broke his vow. When you violate God's law it allows the voice of the thief to become louder and more predominant in your life. "See Samson, these things really don't matter. You touched it and nothing has changed. You can still have God's anointing upon your life. You can still feel His presence and His power. This outward stuff is a bunch of tradition; it's just legalism!"

That voice is still speaking today into the minds and hearts of those who carry the treasure of God's presence upon their lives. I promise you this: it's not always easy to resist the voice because it feels so natural, especially at a weak moment. He will come and whisper, "Look at you. You look so frumpy and plain. Don't you want to stay attractive to your husband? Don't you ever want to find a boyfriend? You would look so much more attractive if you would just 'fix up' a little. People would accept you better at work if you didn't look so different."

I don't know about you, but I'm the first to admit that I'm not always strong. I've had this voice come to me several times and speak its lies while it dangles the sweet taste of the honey before me. It knows exactly the times to attack. It's when you're going through a tough trial, or you're being allowed to sit upon the Potter's wheel and in the process of being broken.

I've had it come and whisper in my ear when I was going through emotional insecurities and changes of life's seasons, which I will share with you later. The only thing I can point to that has been my anchor in life is my true, honest, sincere love for God. I keep coming back to that. I can't make it without God's presence and power in my life. You have to fall in love with Jesus because loving Him is the only thing that's going to keep you safe inside the boat. As Jesus put it:

> If ye love me, keep my commandments
> (John 14:15).

It's the holiness issues that are attacked because satan knows the power that's connected to these sources. When you try to change the laws of God to form around your own opinions and desires, you are headed for disaster and spiritual destruction…it's only a matter of time.

As we see this erosion taking place in the life of Samson, again, he neglects to guard the very source from which his power comes. In Judges 15, when the Philistines came to attack him, Samson reached again for the very thing he was told by God to abstain from – the jawbone of a dead ass.

And when he came unto Lehi, the Philistines shouted against him: and the Spirit of the LORD came mightily upon him, and the cords that *were* upon his arms became as flax that was burnt with fire, and his bands loosed from off his hands. **And he found a new jawbone of an ass,** and put forth his hand, and took it, and slew a thousand men therewith (Judges 15:14,15).

The thief does not steal everything at once.

The Spirit of the Lord was still upon him because it wasn't about the carcass. It wasn't about the jawbone of that donkey. It was about the spiritual connection that was associated with abstaining from what God commanded. It's not really about the actual channels, but it's an attack on the spiritual power that lies behind them and what they represent.

If we don't understand this, if we listen to the voices that tell us it's only a church tradition, or religious standards, or Pentecostal requirements, it will take us down the path Samson traveled. It's a long and winding pathway that takes you to a state of apathy where you will no longer guard or protect one of the most valuable possessions given to you by God. Before you know it, you wake up one day in a world you never thought you would live.

Seven
Using the Weapon of Hatred

Okay, right there I know I lost some of you. Hatred? Did you know that God asks us to 'hate' certain things? God Himself hates specific things. When the emotion of hatred is allowed, it builds up a fortress of defense against the object it is so violently against. Being a "hater" of spiritual deception actually works as a weapon to defend your soul. Read what the Scripture states about it:

> Let those who love the Lord hate evil (Psalm 97:10).

> There is a time to love, and a time to hate
> (Ecclesiastes 3:8).

In Job chapter one, God called Job perfect because he not only "loved God," but also "hated evil."

You may be thinking right now that sounds judgmental or too extreme. You're right; I am extreme. Friend, when you love something with all your heart you don't care who gets offended when it's under attack. It's like when someone attacks or hurts one of your kids, the mama bear can come out of the sweetest and meekest of mothers! You have to get to the place you love this truth in the same manner as you love your kids.

This is not a political viewpoint relationship, where I'm a Republican and you're a Democrat; we can disagree and still be friends. This should be a part of who you are. There is a place you come to where you fall so in love with the God of this truth that it goes far deeper than just a dating relationship to the place you don't want any other spiritual lovers involved. My God is jealous over me, and I want to be as passionate toward Him. It's a love for this truth that consumes you and gets into your spiritual bones and deep into your soul to the place where you become one with it.

This virtue of hatred I'm talking about is not about turning your back on a backslider or to cease from reaching out to them, and please don't walk away from this book thinking that.

I have backslidden friends that I still make visits to their workplaces and use every avenue I have to stay in contact with them in hopes of bringing them back to God. I'm not referring to those who have backslidden. I am referring to those who have purposely walked away from the truth, embraced false doctrine and deception, and are constantly circling the flock of God like wolves trying to pull a lamb out of the fold.

It's the apostates from which you have to distance yourself and your family. You have to be careful of those who have once known this truth. It's those who have once embraced it and then turned and walked away that will come to deceive. There are some things that you can agree to disagree about and still remain in a friendship, but doctrine and holiness is not one of them.

Growing up, I had a friend who became more like the sister I never had. We were very close. All through junior high and high school, we were inseparable. We went to youth events together, camps, liked the same guys; she was always at my house or I was at hers. It was a very close-knit friendship.

After we graduated from high school, I moved from Oklahoma to California to attend Christian Life College in Stockton, and she went on to attend some university. We kept in contact as much as we could with our busy schedules, but eventually our roads took us down separate paths.

One day, I received an email from her. She had gotten married and was filling me in on her married life until the middle of her email when she said, "Kim, I need to tell you something. I no longer believe this way of life. I still love God and still go to church, but I have been set free from the bondage the Oneness Pentecostal Church brought to my life. I no longer believe all that 'stuff that was preached to us' is really necessary. I have a relationship-based commitment now. I look different than what I used to look, and I just wanted you to know."

When I read her email that day I felt like a thousand knives had stabbed through my heart. I sat there stunned, numb inside, with tears streaming down my face. As I sat I took a trip down memory lane and remembered the times she and I would pray and weep at the altar together. I remembered the times we would get so touched by God and one of us would start shouting and then the other would shout too. It was more to me than just a sad choice she made because that choice for me meant the death of a friendship. When you remove the very core of who you are inside, there is nothing left in common but old memories.

I shot one email back to her saying, "I'm so sorry you have made this choice. I love you very much, but I love this truth more than anything else." It was the last time we communicated, and I have never contacted her since then. Only about three years ago another friend of mine had connected with her through social media. She said, "Kim, she doesn't believe anything anymore. I don't think she even goes to any type of church. She is so lost in confusion."

The choice my friend made bonded her with a spirit. My choice bonded me with another Spirit. According to the Word these two worlds cannot walk in unity.

> Amos 3:3 says,
> Can two walk together, except they be agreed?

When you fall in love with the truth, there is something that is birthed inside of you that produces a deep and devoted love for the God of truth.

This produces and creates a passionate resistance (aka hatred) toward anything or anyone who would challenge or defy it. It's not because I think I'm better or more spiritual than someone else, but there is an undying loyalty to this precious truth that divides me from anyone who would deny or stand against it. It's inside of me, it's a part of me, and it's who I am.

You tread very dangerous ground when you fellowship with someone who has fallen into deception because there are spirits that work with them and through them that you cannot see. Parents, you better take note of who you're allowing in your home and having fellowship with.

You may be able to handle it, but your kids will not. It may not entice you, but it will be after your children. Satan will laugh, and talk about, and brag about how he tricked your Pentecostal kid. That's why the Apostle Peter said you better KNOW the devices of the devil! I have watched families, who refused to disfellowship another family member who had fallen into apostasy, weep and travail when that spirit of deception tried to trap their kids. They look back now and wish they had done things differently. As parents, we have to watch over our lives and be careful who we listen to and run with because that spirit is after our children.

I have looked my kids in the eyes on several occasions and told them, "Mychail, Kailah, Joshua, Giahna, and Aunalee, I promise you satan will bring people into your life that will try to get you to question this doctrine. There will be people who will try to get you to do things that are contrary to the Word of God and to question separation from the world or the things the church stands against. It's all because he knows you are carriers of truth for your generation, and he knows you're powerful! If anyone ever has the boldness to attack your God and speak little remarks against His Word, you better not be some mouse in the corner or some undercover Christian who's afraid to open his mouth! You better go after them and boldly defend your beliefs."

That may shock some of you, but I want my kids to understand this. I want them to be prepared with their spiritual bullets in place and the trigger cocked when that spirit of deception comes around. I want them to be consumed and passionate for their God!

I don't want that voice to come as a surprise to them, and I sure don't want them to be ignorant of it. I pray every day they will have a zeal for their God like Phinehas in Numbers 25. Generation after generation, the Jews have understood this secret. As soon as those Jewish babies pass through the birth canal and enter into this world, those mothers start putting a love in their hearts for truth.

Deuteronomy 6:4 are the very first words a Jewish baby will hear:
Hear, O Israel: the Lord our God is one Lord.

It will not be the last time that child hears this scripture, but it is embedded deep within their soul to where they are willing to fight and die for it. I want to build strong walls of defense into my children and my teenagers to where it becomes a part of them…and in order to prove your love for God, you must learn to hate evil. We must buy the truth and sell it not. Some things are just not for sale, nor ever laid out on the bargaining table.

Eight
He Has No Eyes

It would be a terrible thing to go through life without vision. To be able to hear the birds, but never see their colorful feathers and tiny beaks. To hear your children laughing and playing, but not be able to see their little faces. To be able to smell the fragrance of a rose, but not ever know the beauty of its petals. What would be worse would be to walk in spiritual blindness.

> And he said, Go, and tell this people, Hear ye indeed, but understand not; and see ye indeed, but perceive not. Make the heart of this people fat, and make their ears heavy, and shut their eyes; lest they see with their eyes, and hear with their ears, and understand with their heart, and convert, and be healed (Isaiah 6:9,10).

From what Isaiah tells us, when spiritual blindness is allowed to come upon a person, there is no flow of God's healing. It would be living in a darkness that could not compare with physical darkness. You would live in a world of no hope, and even worse, never realize it.

Spiritual blindness is a place a person comes to where the spirit of the individual is unable to perceive or understand spiritual things.

It's unable to function as it should. The people who fall into spiritual blindness have lost all insight, and they begin to rely on intellect and reasoning alone. Those in spiritual blindness are unable to understand spiritual things and are cut off from the spirit realm, but they don't even realize it. A level of spiritual blindness can come upon those who have never known God, but the worst kind comes upon those who have known the truth of God's Word and have turned away from it.

> And with all deceivableness of unrighteousness in them that perish; <u>because they received not the love of the truth</u>, that they might be saved. And for this cause **God shall send them strong delusion, that they should believe a lie**: That they all might be damned who believed not the truth, but had pleasure in unrighteousness (II Thessalonians 2:10,11).

It's a very scary place to wake up to. The problem is, you never wake up.

Again and again, over and over, Samson neglected to guard the very sources his power came through, until one day he was totally unaware that the channel from which the supernatural power of God flowed had been stolen.

As the scissors of the thief began to cut away at the strands of his hair that represented his covenant with God, the glory of the Lord departed from him.

> And she made him sleep upon her knees; and she called for a man, and she caused him to shave off the

seven locks of his head; and she began to afflict him, and his strength went from him. And she said, The Philistines *be* upon thee, Samson. And he awoke out of his sleep, and said, I will go out as at other times before, and shake myself. **And he wist not that the LORD was departed from him** (Judges 16:19,20).

The thief will eventually take it all.

Don't tell me this outward holiness is not important to God! Don't come to me with your questioning voice, trying to convince me it's not connected with the supernatural flowing in my life!

If it's of such little value, then why do those in apostasy spend so much time trying to convince me I'm in bondage? Why not just leave me alone and let me continue living for God the way I want? The truth is, the spirit of the thief is now working IN them, and they have become satan's tool to lure us to sleep so real bondage can come into our lives.

The enemies plan of attack is to get us so focused on the things we cannot do rather than focusing on the power involved in following God's plan. Look at Adam. He got sidetracked on what he could not do (or could not eat) rather on what he was called to do - and it stole his purpose. Some people never partake in the many blessings God has given to them, but remain focused on what God says not to do. The day Adam and Eve ate of the forbidden fruit they died. How did they die? They were separated from God through lost communion and relationship. When you embrace and reach beyond God's boundaries it always brings spiritual death. Even in the beginning, in the Garden of Eden, God placed boundaries to guard and protect His presence in their lives.

The first thing satan will do is make you question God's boundaries and disguise them as being a form of bondage. He will paint you a very deceptive picture of spiritual slavery so your flesh will desire to take control. Since satan cannot get at God he attacks you. Attacking God's children is his way of getting back at God.

These channels of holiness God has called His people to abstain from are what keep His Spirit flowing inside of our lives. I can't explain them, I don't understand the methods behind them, and I can't say they are always easy, but to exchange a little convenience or fleshly desire for what I possess in the Spirit? Never!

This is the greatest treasure we could possibly possess on this earth, experiencing God's Spirit in the levels we encounter. I owe this heritage to my children, I owe this to my family, and I owe this to my generation.

Once the power of God is cut off in a person's life, read what happens:

> But the Philistines took him, and **put out his eyes**, and brought him down to Gaza, and **bound him with fetters of brass**; and he did grind in the prison house (Judges 16:21).

When a life is void of God's Spirit, when the power of God has been stolen, it brings that individual to a place of spiritual and doctrinal blindness. Letting go of the channels of the supernatural will lead you out there further than you will ever want to go!

We think, "No, not me. I will never leave this truth. This is grounded in me." You don't know what you will do when spiritual blindness is allowed into your life. When you are cut off from the power of God, you are no longer in control of your life anymore. You become a servant to the enemy and live in the bondage spiritual blindness brings.

I have been in active ministry for over twenty-three years. Through the years I have watched fine, young adults enroll in Bible College, sincere and hungry for God as they try to find direction for their lives. They witness the supernatural power of God. I've watched them lay for hours prostrate on the floor in deep travail before God, go through four years of Bible-based training through the Scriptures, and live a life of purity and holiness.

But somewhere in their life, they started listening to a voice that told them holiness was not essential and separation was not a heaven or hell issue, it was only tradition. Or maybe the hook of *offense* snagged them. They entertained thoughts or people in their lives that carried the spirit of deception. Little by little, they began to let go of the channels that connected them to the supernatural realm.

You hear about them a few years down the road and it shocks you! They are attending some generic church where truth is relevant, *if* they even go to church. They don't believe anything anymore.

> Be not deceived; God is not mocked: for whatsoever
> a man soweth, that shall he also reap (Galatians 6:7).

It is a very serious thing to mock God and His ways or His Word. You and I are living in the last days before the rapture of the church where everything that can be shaken is being shaken. Anything that cannot be shaken will remain steadfast and strong.

God knows the hearts of those among His people who really love this truth and holiness. Those that do not, He is exposing them and shaking them loose as we prepare for the coming of the Lord. It excites me to see how God is perfecting His church in this hour like never before. There is no devil in hell that can stop what the church is doing for my Bible tells me:

> Ye are of God, little children, and have overcome them: because greater is he that is in you, than he that is in the world (I John 4:4).

Reverend Lee Stoneking, a prophet of God, international evangelist, as well as our good friend, preached a message a few months ago regarding the spirit of deception we are facing in these last days. He said something I have never heard before, but it opened my eyes to the workings of this deceiving spirit. I want to share this with you:

> It all begins with holiness. Let go of holiness and slowly but surely the doctrine begins to erode. Revelation and deception feel exactly the same because they both come from God. Remember the feeling when God gave you the revelation regarding the Holy Ghost and Jesus' Name baptism? It's the exact same feeling except revelation comes with blessing from God, and deception comes with a curse from God. They feel exactly the same. God says, "You want to believe that? I will help you believe it." He sends a strong delusion that they would believe a lie. They are just as excited about the delusion and lie God sent them as they were about truth in the beginning. They say they feel so free, but it is the freedom of a curse God has sent them.
>
> And with all deceivableness of unrighteousness in

them that perish; <u>because they received not the love of the truth</u>, that they might be saved. And for this cause **God shall send them strong delusion, that they should believe a lie:** That they all might be damned who believed not the truth, but had pleasure in unrighteousness (II Thessalonians 2:10).

My friend, there is nothing out there that can equal this. Nothing. Not only is it a refuge in this wicked world we live in, not only is it a shelter and a fortress and a comfort, but it's the only thing that's going to take us out of here when Jesus comes!

When you stay dedicated to this precious apostolic truth, when you walk in the light of this glorious gospel, there is an anointing and power that rests upon you and shines into the darkness of this world. You are a city set upon a hill. You can let the demonstration of the Spirit of God in power that dwells inside of you through the Holy Ghost be released to this lost and confused world. For you are the chosen ones, the chosen people of God!

Ye are the <u>light of the world</u>. A city that is set on an hill cannot be hid. Neither do men light a candle, and put it under a bushel, but on a candlestick; and it giveth light unto all that are in the house. **Let your light so shine before men**, that they may see your good works, and glorify your Father which is in heaven (Matthew 5:14-16).

Nine
God on Display

This book could not be complete without discussing certain channels of separation our God has specified for His people through His Word.

I want to say right here, this is not a chapter on *do's and don'ts* or a set of rules that have been outlined by the author or a church organization. I have chosen only to discuss certain things God has clarified in His Word as points of separation. God has always required separation from His people. Remember how Samson had certain points of separation that God required of him in order for this certain power of God to rest upon his life? He also has things He requires from His people of the twenty-first century.

Again, there is not always detailed reasoning as to *why* God has chosen these certain channels or conduits, but as long as they are outlined and detailed in the Scriptures, they will work the same way for you and me.

The biggest defeat comes when people are afraid to discuss or openly talk about these channels of separation with their kids. The old ways of, *believe and live this way because I told you to,* or *you should never question or enquire about what you're being taught,* no longer works.

I don't ever want that excuse to become the foundation that I build my belief system upon.

I want my children to understand and know which Scriptures support the stands and views we uphold as God's people. I believe someone is going to receive great revelation and understanding of the power of holiness reading this chapter. I believe with all my heart that someone is going to walk away from this book with a whole new outlook, love, and appreciation for the precious and priceless paths of holiness.

Hair and Spiritual Authority

I want to share a powerful testimony with you regarding the subject we are getting ready to address.

> On Monday, January 19, 2009, I received a call at approximately 1:30p.m. from a man who identified himself as an ambulance driver. He stated my son, Keith Smith, requested him to call and inform me he had been in an automobile accident. I was told it was a minor accident, and Keith was currently having an MRI done but there was no major damage. I thanked him for calling and hung up.
>
> Later, I received a call that Keith was all right but would be kept for observation. I found out the other passengers had suffered a concussion, severely bruised lungs, and other injuries.
> It turned out to be way more than a minor accident. The right rear tire had blown out causing the car to spin as it rolled down a ravine of 486 feet.

After the car stopped, Keith and the other two passengers got out of the car and climbed up the hill. Keith didn't look too good and was told to have a seat on the side of the highway. The ambulance came, and Keith was taken to the Santa Rosa hospital.

I was kept informed of his status. A Sunday School class had anointed a handkerchief and sent it to Keith as a prayer cloth, which he wore under his hospital gown.

We thought Keith would be released the next day, but when Wednesday came Keith started running a fever. Another MRI was done and the results showed a hole torn in his intestines. From there, emergency surgery was scheduled. I received the call that Keith was asking for his mother, so I went home as soon as I got off work, packed some clothes, jumped in the truck, and left for Santa Rosa. It took 7 ½ hours to get there from where I lived. I arrived at 3:30am.

I was allowed in ICU and taken to his room. Once I looked at him, my heart sank. He looked awful. I had no idea he would look like death. I let him know I was there, and he went back to sleep.

The next morning the doctor explained he had removed approximately one foot of his intestines and removed the appendix for precautionary purposes. He observed about three feet of his colon was badly bruised along the whole damaged area. A second surgery was already scheduled for Friday to reopen Keith and possibly perform a colostomy. Keith was still running a fever of about 103, his white blood cell count was showing strong infection, and the medication was not bringing it down.

Thursday night I was talking to my friend who told me about Bro. Stoneking's preaching regarding the power of a woman's uncut hair. He told a story in that service of miracles taking place when a woman reminded God of her covenant with Him. After I hung up with her, I woke Keith up and asked if he remembered Bro. Stoneking preaching on the power of a woman's uncut hair? Keith looked at me and said, "Just do it Mom". Right there in that hospital room, when everything looked impossible and the doctors gave us no hope, in an act of faith I took my hair down and laid it across my son's stomach and prayed for God to heal him.

The next morning, I met the doctor again. He had already visited Keith before I got there. He looked at me with amazement and said, "Keith has drastically improved and the surgery has been cancelled!" I was so excited to hear that because I knew it was nothing but the hand of the Healer. As I walked into Keith's room I witnessed a total transformation. Keith looked as if nothing had ever happened.

Satan would love to steal this spiritual power and authority in our lives! He does not want us to grasp the concept of what happens when a woman, in demonstration of her faith, lays out her covenant before God. Let's take a look at the power of a woman's uncut hair.

In I Corinthians 11:2-16, we find some very clear teaching on the length of a man and woman's hair. Here in this chapter, the apostle

Paul is replying to various questions and problems that are arising within the church in Corinth.

I want to point out here that Paul paid attention first to the matters of the heart before he dealt with the outward separation. In the chapters proceeding up to chapter 11, Paul dealt with envy, strife, and divisions that were taking place in the church. He talked about judgmental attitudes and rebuked them for tolerating sin and for living in sexual immorality.

Again, this verifies that the heart must be right first, and then true holiness can follow. It would be so hypocritical for a woman to have hair to her ankles and be living in adultery or trying to divide a church with her gossiping tongue.

Let's look at I Corinthians 11:3

> But I would have you know, that the head of every man is Christ; and the head of the woman is the man; and the head of Christ is God.
> (I Corinthians 11:3)

This verse introduces us to what we are getting ready to discuss, and it begins with headship. Having uncut hair is meaningless if you do not understand your place in the order of God's divine authority. God (or the eternal, invisible Spirit) is first, Christ (or the manifestation of God in flesh) is second; man is third with the woman being under authority to him.

Ladies, this does not mean we are less important than or inferior to the man; this teaches that we are his responsibility. He is responsible to take care of us, protect us, and provide for us. I'm sure glad God made me a woman!

> Every man praying or prophesying, having his head
> covered, dishonoreth his head. But every woman
> that prayeth or prophesieth with her head
> uncovered dishonoureth her head: for that is even
> all one as if she were shaven (I Corinthians 11:4,5).

Clearly, the coverings that are addressed here are regarding hair. For one, Paul uses the word "shaven" in context with what he was addressing. There is no possible way to "shave" a veil or any kind of head wrap, but you can shave a head of hair. Second, no type of veil or headscarf is being referenced in this passage.

> For if the woman be not covered, let her also be
> shorn: but if it be a shame for a woman to be shorn
> or shaven, let her be covered (I Corinthians 11:6).

Nowhere in these last two verses does it say a woman must put on a covering; it only mentions she must be "covered." If she already has her natural, God-given hair as her covering, she does not need to put anything else on her head.

Dr. Daniel Segraves points out in his book, *Hair Length in the Bible:*

> Verse 5 points out that for the woman to pray or prophesy
> with her head uncovered it is equivalent to her being shaven.
> There is no question about what "shaven" means. A woman
> whose head has been shaven has received an obvious mark
> of shame. According to Deuteronomy 21:10-14, God
> considers the shaving of a woman's head to be a humiliation
> to her. If long uncut hair is her covering, she is automatically

shorn when she cuts it and to be uncovered and to be shorn are identical states.

What about trimming the dead ends off? That's been the biggest hoax on the face of the earth. Hairdressers always want to get hold of a woman of God's hair and cut off the spiritual authority that it represents (which we will discuss later).

Remember, they are under the spirit of the world; the world cannot understand this, neither can they comprehend it. We have to abide by the laws of God and not be shaken by the world's standards.

The end of verse six shows us being shorn or shaven is the same in the eyes of God. The word *shorn* comes from the verb *shear*. In the Greek it translates as *keiro,* which means "to have ones hair cut," whether it's one inch or six inches. The hair is *shorn* if any of it is cut. The word *shame* that is used in that same verse comes from the Greek *aischron,* which means something that is shameful, disgraceful, or even dishonest.

> For a man indeed ought not to cover his head, forasmuch as he is the image and glory of God: but the woman is the glory of the man. For the man is not of the woman; but the woman of the man. Neither was the man created for the woman; but the woman for the man (I Corinthians 11:7-9).

Again, Paul is dealing with headship and divine order. The reason a man should not cover his head, or should not let his hair grow long, is because he is the image and glory of God. The woman, who is also created in the image of God, is the glory of the man.

I teach *Marriage and the Family* class at Christian Life College. I love to teach this class because it's an opportunity to reveal the power of walking in your divine order of authority. I tell it very straight to the young ladies in my classes that whomever you choose to marry you better be willing to submit to that man – saved or unsaved. This is a very serious thing in God's eyes.

Women who are single have an advantage because they can *choose* whom they will submit to when they choose their husband. I cannot understand a woman who would fight to live outside the boundaries of submission whether it's her husband, her pastor, or her father. There is a powerful umbrella of protection that covers you and your household when you choose to live under God's divine order.

> For this cause ought the woman to have power on
> her head because of the angels (I Corinthians 11:10).

Okay my friend, stop right here. This is one of the most powerful verses in the entire New Testament, and so many times I have watched people jump right over it, as if they really don't know what to do with it. If you still need a reason to stop trimming your hair, this verse is it.

Back in verse 8, Paul dealt with the order of creation, or the divine order of authority. Remember, the church in Corinth did not have a New Testament like you and I have today. Every teaching had to be drawn from the books of the Old Testament and while Paul was teaching this to the Corinthian church, he was taking his lessons from the book of Genesis.

> And Adam gave names to all cattle, and to the fowl
> of the air, and to every beast of the field; but for

Adam there was not found an help meet for him (Genesis 2:20).

Adam needed a helper and only a woman could fulfill that need. Watch what happened after Eve came along.

> So God created man in his own image, in the image of God created he him; male and female created he them. And God blessed them, and God said unto them, Be fruitful, and multiply, and replenish the earth, and **subdue it: and have dominion** over the fish of the sea, and over the foul of the air, and over every living thing that moveth upon the earth (Genesis 1:27,28).

Notice here, that God blessed *them* and said unto *them*, not just Adam. He told both Adam and Eve to subdue it. Adam was not the only one who was given authority over the planet, but as a couple they were to subdue and have dominion over everything that was upon the earth.

Take note that this was before Lucifer came on the scene. The woman had not yet been told that she was under man's authority as God has not yet made mention of the man ruling over her.

Genesis chapter one is where Paul is teaching from when he is instructing the Corinthian church. He's saying the woman *should* have power and authority on her head, but she doesn't. This dominion was taken from her during the temptation and fall of mankind. After Adam and Eve ate of the forbidden fruit, a curse came upon each of them.

Let's look at the curse that was placed upon the serpent:

> And the Lord God said unto the serpent, Because thou hast done this, thou art cursed above all cattle, and above every beast of the field; upon thy belly shalt thou go, and dust shalt thou eat all the days of thy life (Genesis 3:14).

Then God turned to the woman and said:

> Unto the woman he said, I will greatly multiply thy sorrow and thy conception; in sorrow thou shalt bring forth children; and thy desire shall be to thy husband, and he shall rule over thee (Genesis 3:16).

The curse that was placed upon the woman included pain during childbirth (thanks Eve), and now she will want to compete in authority with her husband. "Thy desire shall be to thy husband," means she will desire to control and rule over him.

You can definitely see this spirit loose in the world. Women have this unseen force that drives them to compete with men. Last month when we were in Israel, there was a huge riot that was caused by a group of women (who were mostly European and American) who refused to abide by the order of the Wailing Wall. They were called "Women of the Wall." They wanted to prove that they could also become priests, rabbis, and religious elders, or any position that had been reserved for men. It was ugly to say the least, and even the Jewish women detested them.

It was during this time of the curse where Eve *lost* the authority God gave to her in the beginning. The authority to take dominion over and subdue had now been cut off from her due to the curse.

The only place in the Old Testament that we find angels involved with authority was right here in the book of Genesis. Eve was involved with a very powerful fallen angel that deceived her. This deception caused her to enter into transgression, which caused her to lose her authority. Sin and rebellion cut off the authority she once had been given by God over the realm of the Spirit.

When you are born again of the water and of the Spirit, you become a new creature in Christ. As the Bible states it,

> Therefore if any man *be* in Christ, *he is* a new creature: old things are passed away; behold, all things are become new. And all things *are* of God, who hath reconciled us to himself by Jesus Christ, and hath given to us the ministry of reconciliation (II Corinthians 5:17,18).

Jesus Christ paid the price to restore us women to our proper place of spiritual authority. The curse was wiped out when we were reconciled to God. This does not take away from the earthly authority God has orchestrated in our lives. We still are required to be in submission to our husbands, but it restores us to the place of opportunity to step back into the authority that was once given to us in the spirit realm.

> There is neither Jew nor Greek, there is neither bond nor free, there is neither male nor female: **for ye are all one in Christ Jesus.** And if ye *be* Christ's, then are ye Abraham's seed, and heirs according to the promise (Galatians 3:28,29).

Paul is telling us that a woman now has the right to be restored to that place of authority, over the angels, and back into the realm of the Spirit.

> For this cause ought the woman to have **power on her head** because of the angels (I Corinthians 11:10).

To get this authority back there is something that God requires, just like God required things of Samson in order for him to possess this power with God. For a woman to be released to operate in this level of spiritual authority, she has to maintain that distinction from a man with her uncut hair. God said if you want to be restored back into that realm of power and authority, let your hair grow as it was in the beginning.

> Judge in yourselves: is it comely that a woman pray unto God uncovered? Doth not even nature itself teach you, that, if a man have long hair, it is a shame unto him? But **if a woman have long hair, it is a glory to her**: for her hair is given her for a covering. (I Corinthians 11:13-15)

Since the beginning of time, separation is what holiness is all about. When a woman wants to move back into the place of spiritual authority, she must understand there are things that God requires to make this connection. This understanding totally takes care of the veil argument.

According to the Scriptures, wearing a veil does not restore a woman back to her spiritual position because she wears a cloth upon her head. There were no veils in the garden! The Bible specifically states it's a woman's *hair* that represents her covering. It's the natural covering in which we were all born.

The word long hair means hair that is allowed to grow. This includes all nationalities, ethnicities, and every hair type. There will be some whose hair will only grow to their shoulders and other can have hair grow to their ankles, but the clear meaning of this is it's impossible to allow hair to grow and at the same time cut off the ends.

There are some ethnicities that have types of hair that just does not grow long even when they do not cut it. In God's eyes, it doesn't matter how long it grows, just as long as it is uncut. Remember, obedience is better than sacrifice!

And holiness is a sacrifice. Don't you ever doubt this. A sacrifice is something that costs you. Paul wanted us to understand this walk of holiness reflects a sacrificial lifestyle.

> I beseech you (strongly urge, beg you) therefore, brethren, by the mercies of God, that ye present your bodies a **living sacrifice,** holy, acceptable unto God, which is your reasonable service.
>
> And be not conformed to this world: but be ye transformed by the renewing of your mind, that ye may prove what is that good, and acceptable, and perfect, will of God. (Romans 12:1,2)

Not being conformed means I cannot do what is natural. If I choose to do what comes natural I will desire to fit in with the world, but walking in holiness and pleasing God through doing His will does not allow me to fit in with the world.

If you want to stay in the will of God, you must walk this path of holiness.

This revelation is so powerful! It makes me want to live this like never before. It releases me to operate my God-given authority over the powers of hell. Revelation brings understanding, and understanding brings power.

No wonder satan doesn't want us to get ahold of this. No wonder he has deceived God's people for years to think it's just a rule or display of modesty. No wonder satan tries to send people into our lives to deceive us of this power! When a woman lets her hair grow, the angelic world stands at attention and takes notice as she steps back into that level of authority and is given power to deal with things in the realm of the Spirit. A woman who cuts or trims her hair is not able to partake of this power in the realm of the supernatural.

Several years ago there was a precious woman of God who believed in the power of a woman's uncut hair. This woman had a daughter who had been raised in church, but as she grew older she walked away from God and gave herself to the world. This woman's daughter got mixed up with the wrong crowd as the spirit of homosexuality got ahold of her, and she became a lesbian.

It was during the preaching of the Word that something happened. My husband began to teach on the power of a woman's prayers when she is under obedience to the Word of God regarding her hair.

This woman got up from her seat, walked down the aisle to the altar and began to pull out bobby pins of every size, shape, and color. She didn't care what anyone else thought as her long, gray hair fell down over the altar, as she laid it out before God. As she began to weep and sob over the soul of her daughter, she reminded God, "God, I'm laying my hair out before You because I want You to see it. This has been my commitment to You. I've honored You, and I have honored Your Word."

This woman had been raised in the truth and brought up in a preacher's home. She had never understood the power that she possessed because it was just a "do" and "don't" commitment. God gave her complete revelation that night, and she realized there was a powerful weapon she had not yet used against the enemy.

Just weeks before this she had tried talking with her daughter about God, but the daughter refused to listen. She had been offended because she wanted to bring her 'partner' over for Thanksgiving dinner, but the godly parents would not allow it. I will never forget the service when a week later in walked two women, one being the woman's daughter and the other the girl's partner who looked like a guy.

This was the daughter who vowed she would never go back to church. When that mother laid her hair upon the altar and reminded God of her covenant with Him, she put into action that spiritual authority over those evil and perverse spirits that bound her daughter. God honored the prayers of that mother and moved upon her child. Within about three months time, her daughter split up with that lesbian partner and totally surrendered her life back to God. Still to this day she lives a pure, clean godly life because a mother used this power that comes with obedience toward a hopeless situation!

The word *power* in I Corinthians 11:10 translated in the Greek is *exousia*, which means, *the power of rule. The power of him whose will and commands must be submitted to by others and obeyed. Authority.*

As women who are under obedience to God, we have the ability to do something the men cannot do. This is what people feel when they step inside of our churches; this spiritual authority coupled with sound doctrine is what sets us apart from all the others. It allows and enables God to release His anointing, His power, and His presence among us.

Dr. Segraves says this:

> A woman who submits to her authority and who displays that submission by her long hair enjoys protection from evil spirits bent on her destruction and also enjoys the benefits that accrue to the people of God. In this way her long hair is 'power' on her head, power against evil and for good.

> A rebellious woman does not have this power. (See I Samuel 15:23.) And a woman who is submissive in spirit but who through ignorance lacks the outward sign of that submission at the least confuses matters in the spirit realm.

Let's look at verse 16:

> But if any man be contentious, we have no such custom, neither the churches of God
> (I Corinthians 11:16).

There are those who would take all fourteen verses that Paul just took time to lay out and try to explain them away with this one verse. Some would claim that Paul was saying if you don't agree with what I just said, you could do what you want. It's ignorant to think that. Why would he take all the time and space to teach on powerful matters only to disregard it if the people didn't agree? Also, why would God divinely inspire Paul to write all this and then turn around and terminate it?

Notice, he was addressing those who were *contentious*. Contention is not of God for it is pride. "Only by pride cometh contention: but with the well advised is wisdom" says Proverbs 13:10. Those who stood against this teaching were considered proud. Yes, they had those people back then, too.

Another common argument that people will use is that Paul was only dealing with a local situation and culture of his day, and that it does not apply to us today. It is plainly revealed in I Corinthians 1:2 that Paul wrote this letter not only to those who were in Corinth, but to "all that in every place call upon the name of Jesus Christ."

How can someone actually believe that all fifteen verses were written just to fill space? Jesus said, "Man shall not live by bread alone, but by every word that proceedeth out of the mouth of God" (Matthew 4:4).

What did God mean when He said,

> All scripture is given by inspiration of God, and is profitable for doctrine, for reproof, for correction, for instruction in righteousness (II Timothy 3:16).

Through the years I have watched saints of God sort through the preached Word of God as if it were the Home Town Buffet. The things that they liked and that were easy to apply to their lives they would take and put on their plate, but the things they didn't want to conform to or accept, were rejected.

Be aware of your influence upon your children. For if a mother becomes rebellious in this divine order, she will transmit her rebellion to her children and their generation will become even more rebellious than hers.

I was counseling with a young woman whose family goes back several generations in Pentecost. She was concerned and burdened about several of her siblings who were raised in the church but were now believing and embracing these crazy, off the wall, doctrinal beliefs. I will never forget what she said. She looked at me with tears in her eyes and said, "Sis. Haney, I have gone back in time and searched my mind to the years spent in our home. I have tried with everything in me to trace what went wrong. What was it that would cause a Pentecostal young person to be so led astray and become so blinded and spiritually disoriented?" With a passion and sorrow in her voice she said, "I can point you to the time when all this confusion entered our home. It was when my mother started cutting and trimming her hair. It made a huge impression on me as a young lady, and I've never forgotten that!"

It's not just about you and me, but there is a supernatural covering that covers our families and our homes when the power of God is allowed to be channeled through our lives. I don't know about you, but I have to have this.

I'm raising five kids in this god-less culture. This is not the same world you and I grew up in as satan's forces have been released without restraint in these last days. Like never before we are fighting spiritual forces of hell that have been targeted at the church. We are going to challenge this attack of hell with an apostolic authority as we stand before the enemy with the power that flows through our committed lifestyle and the authority it releases in the realm of the spirit.

The little things we allow can produce something in the hearts of our kids that can grow into monsters down the road. I know my kids think I'm old fashioned and a little extreme at times, but I have to remain strong in order to balance the pull and the weight this world has upon them.

We have to place our trash cans out by the street the night of our neighborhood pick up days. One evening, after the sun had already gone down, my daughter Kailah was asked to wheel the trash can to the street. She had already gotten dressed for bed and had her sweat pants on. She asked, since nobody would technically "see" her since it was already dark outside, if she could just run the trash out to the curb in her sweats. My first reply was yeah, go ahead, but then I caught myself. What kind of signal was I sending to my daughter? Maybe nobody would see her out there in her sweats, but *she would know it*, and God would know it. I have been placed in her life as a sounding board and a router to lead and direct her to do the right things and to live her life pleasing to God everyday and in every circumstance. It's all or nothing with God.

I went to her before she walked out and suggested she put a skirt on to take the trash out. Little signals that seem so insignificant at the time can become so impressionable in their lives and cause major repercussions.

I think of a family who allowed their little girls to wear girly nail polish and "cute" little jewelry when they were small and now their girls are older and are so distant to God. They come to church, sit on the pew next to their parents and remain as cold as a corpse in the presence of God. The cute painted nails and little adorable pieces of jewelry have now turned into boy-short hair, gaudy earrings, and a lifestyle of rebellion and worldliness.

My kids will be most influenced by me. How close I walk with God will effect the way they walk with God. I cannot get around this, nor can I deny it. When I chose to bring five children into this world I also stepped into a great responsibility in the eyes of God.

Gilda Radner was a Jewish-American comedian and actress who died of ovarian cancer in 1989. In her book, *It's Always Something*, she tells the touching story of a dog and her housekeeper/nanny named Dibby:

> When I was little, Dibby told me a story about her cousin who had a dog – just a mutt – and the dog was pregnant. I don't know how long dogs are pregnant, but she was due to have her puppies in about a week.
> She was out in the yard one day and got in the way of the lawnmower and her two back legs got cut off. They rushed her to the vet who said, "I can sew her up, or you can put her to sleep if you want. But the puppies are OK – she'll be able to deliver the puppies.
>
> Dibby's cousin said, "keep her alive." So the vet sewed up her backside and over the next week that dog learned how to walk. She didn't spend any time worrying; she just learned to walk by taking two steps in the front and flipping up her backside and then taking two more steps and flipping up her backside again.

She gave birth to six little puppies, all in perfect health. She nursed them and then weaned them. And when they learned to walk, they all walked like her.

Those little puppies, even though they had perfectly strong, normal legs, learned to walk by watching their mother. Never underestimate the power of example. After hearing this touching story, I have thought about the people in my life I walk like, and those who will learn to walk like me.

The illustration of that momma dog and her pups reminds me that my children will learn to walk with God the way I walk with God. If I am weak in certain areas this will be passed on to them, but on the other hand, when I choose to stand strong, this will also become their strengths.

There is no denying it, we are swimming against the current in our culture. It is not popular nor is it common to see men, women and youth who are totally sold-out to a God they cannot see. Religion has become only a denomination or a social club in America.

I wish every Christian could take at least one trip to Israel to encounter the absolute, sold-out passion of the jewish people. Their lives are centered around their God, their prayer lives, the text, and coming of Messiah. Sports are rarely heard of and if they are instituted at all, it is only for exercise. Every time I visit the Holy Land I am encouraged by a people who live their lives so totally consumed by God in an atmosphere where separation is not only accepted, but embraced. I am also reminded that I have something greater inside of me - I have what they are seeking. I have the literal Spirit of God living inside of me to help me buck the current of this wicked society. I have a God who speaks to me, visits me, strengthens me, and consumes every corner of my life. As my dear father-in-law always said, "It's easy to live for God hard, but it's hard to live for God easy."

I don't want to be responsible for breaking down the channels of separation in my kid's lives! They may call me old fashioned, but deep inside they are thankful for a mother who is neither afraid to stand against the waves of spiritual destruction nor bow to the popularity and pressure of the culture. When you plant seeds of righteousness and godliness into the fertile soil of your young children's hearts, I promise you mother, it will take root and begin to grow for itself one day. We only have one chance, or one shot at planting seeds of righteousness into the soil of our children's hearts.

I now have a twenty year old daughter that comes to me and wants to know if something she is wearing is too short, too tight, too shear, etc. because she now has it for herself. When you have done all you can do, you can remind God of His promise:

> Train up a child in the way he should go: and when
> he is old, he will not depart from it (Proverbs 22:6).

But we still have to TRAIN. Sunday School can't do this. Christian schools can't do this. Taking them to church is not enough. We have to teach and pass down to our children this heritage of righteousness.

I Corinthians 11:10 tells me as a woman there is power on my head because of the angels. When a woman does not cut her hair, she walks in a realm of the spirit that is absolutely miraculous.

Everywhere I go, I am anointed by God, and I have the presence of angels in my life. The world around me feels it!

There's been too many times I have been so overwhelmed with heavy burdens, times my husband has been sick unto death, and when nobody was home I would take my hair down and hold up the split ends to God and remind Him this is my covenant with YOU!

I have gotten on my knees and laid my uncut hair over my husband's cowboy boots or one of my kid's shoes or pictures and *felt* the electrifying flow of God's Spirit rush over me and through me with a power that is not of this world!

I have witnessed God's divine intervention as I have watched Him stop planes, change schedules, send angels to interfere with satan's plans, change the heart of a judge, intervene in the decisions of juries, and shut the voices of attackers. I have felt the presence of angels more times than I can count. They have ministered to me when no one was around; they have brought messages of warning when the enemy conspired against me. The angels of God have helped me and worked on my behalf because they can look and see a woman who is under authority by taking note of my uncut hair.

I have felt the powerful presence of these angels many times in our church services as the supernatural begins to manifest and all of glory descends as people fall on their faces before God. I feel the presence of God's angels right now as I'm writing, and it makes me want to cry; it makes me want to get on my face and worship! It makes me want to lift my hands and thank God for this wonderful revelation. It makes me want to embrace this treasure of God's presence and understand that I am chosen by Him! If we can ever wake up to who we really are and what it is we have hold of, it will transform our lives.

I can't image living without this. Refusing to cut my hair is small price to pay in regards to the great rewards that accompany it.

If you are a single woman reading this, I want to tell you that God will fulfill every need in your life, including your financial needs, when you seek Him first and honor His ways. I want to share Megan's testimony:

> I was someone who had grown up on a church pew and had been taught my entire life to not cut my hair. I stood behind what I had been taught but never really understood *why* I did not cut it.
>
> A few years back I attended a Ladies Advance Conference in Stockton, California, and heard a message regarding the power of a woman's uncut hair. During that message, I received something special; I received a true revelation for myself on the power submission brings upon my life and my family when I submit my hair to God. It was so powerful! The floodgates of understanding just poured open in my mind. I will never forget what I felt during that service.
>
> A while after that conference, my husband and I were facing some very serious financial situations. The debt seemed to be snowballing into a mountain and I began to worry and let fear and anxiety take hold of me. Night after night I was unable to sleep, pacing the hallways of our home, trying to figure out a plan of how I could fix this problem that had

come our way. I prayed and I fasted. I pleaded with God but no miracle came and the bill collectors were knocking. I began to wonder if my prayers were even being heard.

One early morning I sat down in our living room, hoping to figure out a plan of how we could pay our bills for the month. We were short exactly $500 and there seemed absolutely no way out. I told no one about this amount we owed, but continued to take it to God everyday.

I felt impressed to go pick up my entire stack of bills. They seemed so overwhelming as I looked down at them in my hands. As I began to lift them up to God, I was reminded of the message regarding the power of a woman's uncut hair. I began to remove my pins and let my hair down as I laid my hair over that stack of bills and prayed.

The next morning I came to work and went into my office. I noticed an envelope lying on my desk and as I reached to open it I uncovered a check for exactly $500. I just could not believe it! I went to thank the couple whose name was on the check and they explained to me that the Lord had laid that exact amount of money upon their hearts. Neither one of them knew what the other was thinking as they were amazed how God had directed them separately to give this amount.

God watches over and protects those who commit their lives to Him! There is more to this thing than just the Holy Ghost experience. There is more than just going to church on Sunday mornings and trying to live a good life. Jesus wants to consume us and become the source of every need we will ever have. There is something magical that happens when we surrender our flesh and our body to His will. It opens the door for us to walk in a greater realm of the Spirit filled with miracles and provisions that accompany obedience.

Ten
The Power of the Fig Leaf

I have watched many people come and go from our church altars. Many of them come from various churches that do not teach or understand separation from the world in views of modesty and holiness, but they are very sincere. I have watched, when the Holy Ghost comes upon them for the first time, they receive a supernatural encounter with God that they have never felt before.

At Christian Life Center, we make it a practice to never shove anything down someone's throat, but allow God to work at His own pace in that person's life as they hear the teaching and the preached Word. Time after time I have had women come to me saying they just didn't feel right about certain clothing items they used to wear, or they put it on and just felt the tug of a little small voice inside say *no.*

Honestly, I have been in my own closet and put on a skirt or a piece of clothing and felt that inner voice say *I don't think so.* Maybe I had gained a little weight since I wore it last, or it was something that made me feel "sexy" even though it was long enough and high enough. If you are a female, you know what I mean. You can find skirts to the floor that show every curve in your body and leave nothing to the imagination. I have a little compact mirror in my purse, and when I try on a skirt in the dressing room I take that mirror out to see what that outfit looks like from behind. I know that sounds crazy, but I've seen some women that *need* to bring a mirror when they go shopping.

Let's face it: the world pulls at us to look accepted by their standards, but sometimes it's not always the world. We can become our worst enemies when we try to compete with others around us. I have told my own girls, as well as the young ladies in the Christian Life College classes I teach, that you have to choose to either be godly or sexy; you cannot be both. Every Christian woman comes to this decision in her life and her choice will determine her path.

When a person is never willing to pay the cost of commitment, their whole life becomes a facade. This whole Christian walk becomes a fake or a front, and as you get older you will never be able to look back and see what you could have been for God because the cost on the price tag of commitment you never were willing to pay.

We all want to look skinny, healthy, in shape, have flawless skin, perfect white teeth, thick hair, a gorgeous wardrobe, and feel attractive, but there is a fine line you can easily cross. When you are constantly measuring yourself against the magazine ads, celebrities, and women of the world, you can easily lose sight of what your purpose is, Whom you're separated unto, and Whom you serve. You have to set boundaries in your life that will help keep your eyes focused on what your purpose is on this earth.

Here again we are back at the center of it all: our hearts. Every choice I make represents a step that will either take me closer to my Jesus, or it will lead me further away from Him.

If you live for God for very long, you will eventually come to the place where you will question why. Why are we different? Why do we believe and live by these certain standards of holiness? These questions don't always come from a negative standpoint, but from curiosity and a hunger to know. Knowledge is power and knowing the things you believe and stand for are what God desires of us, releasing us to operate in the power it provides.

Modest Clothing

Why do we dress the way we do? Let's take a look at the very beginning. Adam and Eve have just eaten of the forbidden fruit, and they are feeling shame:

> And the eyes of them both were opened, and they knew that they were naked; and they sewed fig leaves together, and made themselves aprons (Genesis 3:7).

Before they ate the fruit that God told them not to eat, they ran around the garden naked, clothed with nothing, and they had no shame. Kind of reminds me of the water parks throughout this nation. They did not feel badly about this nor did they try to run behind every tree to cover their bodies.

When they disobeyed God and sin entered into the world, they realized that having no clothes brought shame and disgrace. They now realized they were in a shameful state of being.

Do you know what they did to try to fix the shame and embarrassment they were feeling? They found some fig leaves, which are very large, and began to sew them together to make themselves a covering to clothe their flesh. While this was happening, God came looking for them.

I want to point out something right here; God knew they had sinned. He knew they were feeling this shame and humiliation, but He kept reaching for Adam and Eve. God didn't cut off His search or desire for visitation with them once they sinned and made a mistake, but the Lord called for Adam even after he sinned and disobeyed.

Don't ever let the enemy tell you God has rejected you, pushed you aside, or doesn't love you anymore because you made a mistake. Most of all God wants fellowship and relationship with His people, and He seeks for those intimate moments with His children every day.

I want to share something very powerful: Eve was formed from the rib of Adam to be a companion, friend, help meet, and created for intimate relationship (Ladies, I guess we could Scripturally justify we are God's gift to men ... only kidding). Just as Eve was taken from Adam's rib to fulfill this need, the church (you and I) were created from the wounded side of the second Adam (Jesus Christ) for the very same reason - to have intimate fellowship and companionship. Jesus wants a relationship with His children!

> And the Lord God called unto Adam, and said unto him, Where art thou? And he said, I heard thy voice in the garden, and I was afraid, because I was naked; and I hid myself (Genesis 3:9,10).

We just read back in verse 7 where Adam and Eve tried to sew fig leaves together to make them a garment, but now he's confessing to God that he's naked and trying to hide. Obviously, the fig-designed outfit was inadequate. I'm sure Adam did what he could, but apparently his outfit did not cover his body decently enough to stand in God's presence because he still felt the marks of shame. He and Eve were still hiding in the bushes from God because they understood now that their bodies must be clothed in a certain way in order for them to come into the presence of a holy, Almighty God.

So what did God do about this situation? He made them clothes that were suitable for Him.

> Unto Adam also and to his wife did the Lord God
> make coats of skins, and clothed them
> (Genesis 3:21).

God got intricately involved when it came time to choose clothing. It sure makes you wonder what they looked like (Versace watch out!).

What's so powerful about this is we only have two accounts where God Himself made something with His own hands: the creation of Adam and the clothing He made for Adam and Eve to wear. Don't tell me clothing and modesty doesn't matter to God! The fact that the Master of the Universe would be so concerned and involved in the way His children were clothed tells me it's important. God takes two innocent animals, which meant bringing death to members of His own creation, in order to clothe mankind properly.

God cares how we clothe our bodies! This story also gives us an understanding of how God and man have different views of what it means to clothe our bodies. This is why we cannot always count on our judgment alone, but we must live our lives according to what is outlined in the Scriptures and what is spoken through our pastor. The Holy Ghost will teach us and show us how to dress as we allow

His holy nature to be demonstrated to this world through our outward appearance.

This does not give us a ticket to dress sloppy, shabby, thrown together, outdated, or homely. In fact, it should do quite the opposite. Knowing that we may be the only representation of Jesus the world ever sees means we should dress with an air of royalty. Not with expensive, gaudy, outlandish clothing, but with style, class and a sense of dignity and honor because we belong to the King. You are daughters of the King of Kings!

Okay, I'm standing really tall right now on my soapbox. I will be honest with you; I cringe inside when I see a Christian woman dressed like she just crawled out of bed. Holiness should make us dress *better* than what we dressed in the world.

There is a sweet older lady in my church that, every time I see her, she is decked out from head to toe and wearing higher heels than I wear. She told me that she dressed up when she was in the world, and when she came to Jesus she made up her mind she was going to represent Him better than she did the god of the world. I commend her! It does not require a fat bank account to dress nicely; we have incredible thrift stores and resale shops that clothe most of my family. Make it a priority to look your best when you're out in public because you represent Jesus Christ to this world. When your godly spirit is paired up with your godly, yet classy, outward appearance what a powerful tool of witness! It will make others want to be a Christian and live for this Jesus you serve.

Okay, I crawled off my soapbox.

Let's take a look at what modest clothing is referred to and God's outlook on jewelry. In I Timothy, Paul is teaching a young minister what to teach others. In verse 9 he shifts his focus to the women of the church.

> In like manner also, that women adorn themselves in modest apparel with shamefacedness and sobriety; not with broided hair, or gold, or pearls, or costly array; But (which becometh women professing godliness) with good works.
> (I Timothy 2:9,10).

Let's dissect the words modest apparel. What defines the term modest? Modest means, "without excess of any kind, moderate and discreet." So if our apparel is to be moderate and discreet what defines the word *apparel*?

Reverend Eli Lopez, who is Pastor Haney's right hand man, taught an amazing lesson on what true, modest apparel was revealed in I Timothy 2. He had extensively researched this subject, and I have asked his permission to share this revelation and understanding with you. I offer my deepest thanks to Bro. Lopez for his spiritual insight in this subject.

> The word *apparel* comes from the Greek word *katastole,* which is only used once in the Scriptures. Paul could have chosen several terms to describe the word *apparel,* but this specific word was chosen because it has such significance behind it.

> It comes from a derivative of the Greek word *stole. A stole* is a stately robe. Examples of a *stole* in the bible was the robe that clothed the prodigal son when he came back to his

father's house, the robes the religious scribes wore, and the precious robes of the glorified saints mentioned in Revelation 7:9.

These were not just your everyday bathrobes. These were stately robes of distinction; not only were they stately, but they had great significance. The word *katastole* means a long, special, robe-like garment that covers the body. The Hebrew and Greek Study Bible written by Greek scholar, Spiros Zodhiates, states this word *katastole* interprets "a long garment reaching down to the feet." Paul could have chosen any other word to represent modest apparel, but he chose this one to distinctly explain what was trying to be conveyed.

The pattern of clothing that was given to us way back in Genesis is still in effect today. This is why Paul used this specific word when he described how a woman should cover her body.

God told the Jewish people it was an abomination, or something that caused God disgust or hatred, for a woman to wear any item of clothing that is associated with a man. It is unacceptable to God.

> The woman shall not wear that which pertaineth unto a man, neither shall a man put on a woman's garment: for all that do so are abomination unto the Lord thy God (Deuteronomy 22:5).

God hates it so much, He even likens this same abomination to the abomination that takes place in a homosexual relationship.

> Thou shalt not lie with mankind, as with
> womankind: it is abomination (Leviticus 18:22).

I don't know about you, but I don't want anything to do with something God calls an abomination. According to Isaiah 47:2-3, God considers showing your entire leg and uncovering your thigh to be shameful exposure and is also referred to as nakedness in His sight.

> Take the millstones, and grind meal: uncover thy
> locks, make bare the leg, **uncover the thigh**, pass
> over the rivers. Thy **nakedness** shall be uncovered,
> yea, **thy shame** shall be seen: I will take vengeance,
> and I will not meet thee as a man (Isaiah 47:2,3).

This is why Christians do not wear shorts, short skirts or anything above the knee. From the kneecap to the hip is considered the thigh area. Again, that word *katastole* directs us to long dresses or skirts that modestly cover our knees. God has always wanted distinction between the world and His people.

I wish every Oneness believer could save up enough money to take a trip to Israel. I cannot express to you how it will change your life and your outlook on separation and holiness when you can witness the separation of the Jewish people. Honestly, I never liked to travel overseas and made up in my mind I wasn't going to get caught up in the "drama" of going to Israel – until my first trip.

We get so caught up in our Western world to the place we just think everyone lives like we do. But until you take a trip to Israel, it's hard to understand how passionate and sold out the Jews are to Jehovah, Who is the same God you and I serve. They look just like us, or should I say, we look like them?

In June of 2013, when we took our family to Israel, as we were just walking down the sidewalks in Jerusalem the Jewish women would just stare at my girls and me. They knew we were different from the Muslims and also different from other Christian groups, but even more than that I know they felt the Spirit of God flowing through us. It's almost a magical feeling to be over there.

There's an unspoken, inward connection with these people who have been carriers of this precious revelation that we hold dear, "The Lord our God is One Lord." They look different than those who are non-practicing as they are truly joined to the God they serve, heart, soul, mind and body, and it challenges me. Remember, these Jews are the same Jews God addressed as a "Holy people unto the Lord."

> For thou *art* an **holy people unto the LORD thy God**: the LORD thy God hath chosen thee to be a special people unto himself, above all people that *are* upon the face of the earth (Deuteronomy 7:6).

If God required separation through holiness back then for His chosen people, why would He not extend the call of holiness to us? Those who have been called of God, obeyed the Scriptures, and grafted into the vine.

> Thou wilt say then, The branches were broken off, that I might be grafted in (Romans 11:19).

If you have never fully engaged or invested in anything spiritual you cannot understand this. People that try to get things from God that they themselves are not willing to give can never truly understand what it means to be joined to Him. Throughout the entire Old Testament God portrays Israel as being separated and holy as they were made holy *unto Him;* He still requires His people today to be holy.

Let's talk about jewelry

Many churches believe and teach that the Bible is always relevant to the culture. If that were true, it would mean the culture of the world (whatever generation you lived in) would have the power to change the opinion of God and His church. If this were true, there would be nothing in the Bible we could literally apply to our lives, including the doctrine.

> **ALL Scripture** is given by inspiration of God, and is profitable for doctrine, for reproof, for correction, for **instruction in righteousness** (II Timothy 3:16).

When the apostle Paul wrote to Timothy regarding the teachings of the church, he specified certain areas of our lives that perform as channels of separation.

> In like manner also, that women adorn themselves in modest apparel, with shamefacedness and sobriety; **not with broided hair, or gold, or pearls, or costly array** (I Timothy 2:9).

Paul mentioned three things that many first-century women were using to draw undue attention to themselves: braided hair, gold, pearls, and costly clothing.

In the first century, many women were plaiting elaborate hair designs that would take hours to "construct" and weave. Apparently, some women were turning the worship assemblies into fashion shows, attempting to *outdo* their contemporaries with flashy, expensive clothes and costly gold jewelry. Women of that culture would weave gold, pearls, and other types of jewelry throughout their hairstyles in a very gaudy and provocative way. They did this to bring attention to their wealth, status, and to attract the eyes of men.

Since Paul ends verse 9 with costly array, gold, and pearls, they would be seen as independent items aside from the woman's hair. This introduces the gold and pearls mentioned here as jewelry, not just woven strands of gold or pearls in her hair, although it could be another form of wearing jewelry used to attract attention to her flesh instead of portraying godliness.

Paul is telling Christians they are not to dress like the world as he specifies gold, pearls and costly clothing (array). Peter also addressed this issue in I Peter 3.

> Whose adorning let it not be that outward adorning of plaiting the hair, and of wearing of gold, or of putting on of apparel; But let it be the hidden man of the heart, in that which is not corruptible, even the ornament of a meek and quiet spirit, which is in the sight of God of great price (I Peter 3:3,4).

Instead of this gaudiness, Paul instructed the women to adorn themselves in that "which is proper for women professing godliness." When I'm shopping at some department or grocery store and I see one our godly women walking down the aisle, they have a very special glow about them. They are not like the women of the world who let everything hang out. A Christian woman is defined by who she is and Who she is separated unto.

The conservative Jewish women practice something they call *tzniut*, (pronounced tz'neeOOT) which is loosely defined as modesty. They believe that when people separate themselves from worldly dress, it acts as a spiritual catapult that connects them to God.

In her book, *Outside Inside* Gila Manolson, who is a Jewish author, writes this:

> Today, *tzniut* is truly a light in the darkness. For *tzniut* is infinitely more than what we wear – it's who we are. *Tznuit* is the key to all spiritual growth and therefore to a healthy society. Rather than restricting, *tzniut* is, in the most profound sense, liberating. Anything spiritual is difficult to capture in words. *Tznuit,* too, can be truly understood only through witnessing it, or better, living it.

My husband was in Israel a few years ago, and his tour group was headed into one of the Orthodox Jewish communities when their bus came upon a riot. The bus driver had to go around due to all the police that had come to the scene. Later they found out a woman had walked into that neighborhood in immodest western clothing, a pantsuit, and they tried to stone her.

They have signs in their Jewish marketplaces and neighborhood communities that warn those who choose to enter with immodest clothing they will do so at their own risk. Necks, elbows, and legs are not allowed to be shown in public. If a woman were to walk in with pants or a short skirt, they would become extremely angry and probably start throwing items at her. Now I am not affirming their behavior as being right, but why would they do this? Why would they become so violent? Because they believe their God is *holy*. They are a people who believe holiness much stricter and harder than we do, and they are not ashamed of what they believe. They have a deep passion toward their God as they live consumed by the Text.

Now, let's take a look at whom the Scriptures connect with the wearing of jewelry.

In the New Testament, which is the contract God has made with His church, there were three women used as symbols representing three different types of people: the Bride, Israel, and the great whore.

The bride and Israel, who are both chosen by God, do not have any type of jewelry. The woman (or the great whore) who represents apostate Christianity (those who have turned their backs on truth) is mentioned, very interestingly, being *covered in jewelry*.

First, let's look at how God describes His church:

> Husbands, love your wives, even as Christ also loved the church, and gave himself for it; That he might sanctify and cleanse it with the washing of water by the word, That he might present it to himself a glorious church, not having spot, or wrinkle, or any such thing; but that it should be holy and without blemish (Ephesians 5:25-27).

The bride of Christ, or the church, is described as being holy and without blemish:

> And round about the throne *were* four and twenty seats: and upon the seats I saw four and twenty elders sitting, <u>clothed in white raiment; and they had on their heads crowns of gold</u> (Revelation 4:4).

The four and twenty elders here represent the church that has been raptured. The Bible describes the Bride of Christ as being clothed only in white raiment (purity) and having crowns of gold upon their heads. There is no mention of jewelry being displayed on the people of God.

Now let's read how the great whore is depicted:

> So he carried me away in the spirit into the wilderness: and I saw a woman sit upon a scarlet coloured beast, full of names of blasphemy, having seven heads and ten horns. <u>And the woman was arrayed in purple and scarlet colour, and decked with gold and precious stones and pearls</u>, having a golden cup in her hand full of abominations and filthiness of her fornication (Revelation 17:3,4).

It's amazing that this filthy woman is being vividly described as wearing jewelry. She is also the *only one* out of the three who is mentioned being decked with jewelry. This is not describing a sinner or someone who has never known God or the truth of His Word, but this woman is representing the apostate church, those who have once known truth and have chosen to walk away and believe a lie.

If you live for God long enough you will encounter those who will talk about the "liberty" they have since they walked away from holiness. This is the same line they were using 2,000 years ago during the apostles' day. Like the same old line used by the drunks in the bars, "Haven't I met you before?"

Peter writes about these people:

> While they promise them liberty, they themselves are the servants of corruption: for of whom a man is overcome, of the same is he brought in bondage. For if after they have escaped the pollutions of the world through the knowledge of the Lord and Saviour Jesus Christ, they are again entangled therein, and overcome, the latter end is worse with them than the beginning.
> For it had been better for them not to have known the way of righteousness, than, after they have known it, to turn from the holy commandment delivered unto them (II Peter 2:20,21).

It's always amazing to hear those who are entwined in the most bondage speak of liberty. How can they give what they don't have? Their so-called "liberty" is hiding behind the mask of deception and their freedom is actually the bondage they have embraced because of their failure to love the truth.

Again, this is not talking about sinners. The spirit of apostasy can only rest upon those who have once known holiness, true doctrine, and been filled with the Holy Ghost.

> For *it is* impossible for **those who were once enlightened,** and have tasted of the heavenly gift, and were **made partakers of the Holy Ghost,** And have tasted the good word of God, and the powers of the world to come, <u>If they shall fall away</u>, to renew them again unto repentance; seeing they crucify to themselves the Son of God afresh, and put *him* to an open shame (Hebrews 6:4-6).

Obviously, the wearing of jewelry is an outward reflection of what this woman represents. Amazingly, God chose jewelry to convey one of the signs of spiritual adultery and blasphemy. The point is this: I never want to imitate or mirror a symbol of what those in apostasy represent.

Why am I analyzing and exploring all these subjects? Because we need to know for ourselves. We must know the things that please God and what does not please Him. We must know what the Scriptures teach! Satan takes advantage of Scripturally ignorant people who sincerely love God but do not have a leg to stand on when the serpent comes around and throws questions their way.

Let's take a look at make-up

Three times the Bible makes reference to makeup. Each time it's mentioned in connection with a harlot or a very wicked and perverse woman. It's also connected with God's people when they were in a backslidden state and gives us insight on how God feels about it.

Let's look at the first mention of make-up:

> And in the eleventh year of Joram the son of Ahab began Ahaziah to reign over Judah. And when Jehu was come to Jezreel, Jezebel heard of it; and **she painted her face**, and tired her head, and looked out at a window (II Kings 9:29,30).

Jezebel was probably the most wicked woman ever mentioned in the Bible. She was associated with immorality, the murder of God's prophets, prostitution, and idolatry, and she was specifically known for painting her face. According to the Egyptian customs, this would have mostly included her eyelashes and her eyelids.

The writer of this passage could have just told us she looked out at a window. He did not have to include the details of her painting her face if that fact was not important for us to grasp. Without exception, every example of make-up in the Bible is associated with wicked and godless women.

Applying eye makeup, which was called khol, often connected to flirting in Hebraic thinking. Isaiah 3:16, Jeremiah 4:30, Ezekiel 23:40, and Proverbs 6:24–26 provide examples of women who bat their painted eyes to lure innocent men into adulterous beds.

Black kohl was an ancient eye cosmetic, traditionally made by grinding lead sulfide and other ingredients. It was widely used to darken the eyelids and as mascara for the eyelashes. It is incorporated in Bible passages as a symbol of feminine deception and trickery, and it was used to paint the area above and below the eyelids and is generally considered part of a woman's arsenal of artifice.

In Jezebel's case, however, the cosmetic is more than just an attempt to accentuate the eyes. Jezebel is donning the female version of armor as she prepares to do battle. She is a feminine woman warrior, waging war in the only way a woman can.

The times when Israel was backslid and had turned their backs on God, the Scriptures portrayed their backslidden state with a woman who painted her face and eyes.

Let's look at Jeremiah 4:30:

> And when thou art spoiled, what wilt thou do? Though thou clothest thyself with crimson, though **thou deckest thee with ornaments of gold, though thou rentest thy face with painting,** in vain shalt thou make thyself fair; thy lovers will despise thee, they will seek thy life (Jeremiah 4:30).

> And furthermore, that ye have sent for men to come from far, unto whom a messenger was sent; and, lo, they came: for whom thou didst wash thyself, **paintedst thy eyes,** and deckedst thyself with ornaments (Ezekiel 23:40).

Painting the eyes was connected with harlots and was evidence that a woman had loose morals. Solomon warned his son to stay clear of these types of women:

> To keep thee from the evil woman, from the flattery
> of the tongue of a strange woman. Lust not after her
> beauty in thine heart; **neither let her take thee with
> her eyelids**. For by means of a <u>whorish woman</u> a
> man is brought to a piece of bread: and the adultress
> will hunt for the precious life (Proverbs 6:24-26).

The Bible always associates makeup with wrong values and a backslidden heart, and it never speaks favorably about it. Be aware of the subtle attacks of the thief! Guard the channels in your life that allow the presence of God to flow.

My friend, God leads us by His Spirit to become separate, but I'm not stupid or blind; I know it's not always the easiest thing to turn away from fleshly desires. This is why your walk with God, your consistent relationship with Him, is the core and strength that is going to keep you living a life that is not only pleasing to Jesus but will remain powerful.

Because of what's taking place right now in the spirit realm, you no longer can just live off your altar experiences. You can't live for God from Sunday to Sunday and live in the power of His Spirit the way He has purposed us to live. I challenge you today, give your all to God. Give Him your insides, your guts, your whole heart, your spirit, your innermost being, and your body.

> I beseech you therefore, brethren, by the mercies of
> God, that ye **present your bodies** a living sacrifice,
> holy, acceptable unto God, which is your reasonable
> service (Romans 12:1).

I promise you this, when you live a committed life unto the Lord, you will walk in the spirit of such liberty and freedom. It releases you into a relationship with Jesus Christ that can be obtainable through no other method than the beautiful spirit of holiness. As the glory of God manifests, it flows through the pipeline of holiness. This is the most valuable possession on the face of this earth, and I want to guard and protect the glory of the Lord in my life.

Eleven
Obedience opens the Floodgate of Blessing

None of us are perfect, and I will place my name at the top of the "imperfection" list. Never would I want to conclude or suggest that God "punishes" us because we aren't perfect, but it is true that God is not obligated to *bless us* when we don't trust and obey Him. There is a difference. As Psalm 84 and many other passages of Scripture confirm, when we obey the Lord we are under the glory spout where the glory pours out. When we don't trust and obey God, we give the devil power and authority in our lives as the thief comes to steal, kill, and destroy.

What did God promise the Israelites in Deuteronomy 28 if they listened to His voice and obeyed His commands? *"All these blessings shall come on thee, and overtake thee."*

> And it shall come to pass, if thou shalt hearken diligently unto the voice of the LORD thy God, to observe *and* to do **all his commandments** which I command thee this day, that the LORD thy God will **set thee on high above** all nations of the earth: And all these blessings shall come on thee, and overtake thee, if thou shalt hearken unto the voice of the LORD thy God (Deuteronomy 28:1-2).

I don't know about you, but I need God's blessings in my life. What comes to your mind when you think of God's blessings? Many times we think of answered prayers, finding a check in the mailbox when we needed to pay rent, gaining favor during a job interview, driving a nice car, having a closet full of beautiful clothes, or having healthy children. The idea of blessing is usually connected with what our needs are at the moment.

God has promised to bless His children who obey and trust Him, even when He does not make sense.

> And why call ye me, Lord, Lord, and **do not the things which I say**? Whosoever cometh to me, and heareth my sayings, **and doeth them**, I will shew you to whom he is like: He is like a man which built an house, and digged deep, and laid the foundation on a rock: and when the flood arose, the stream beat vehemently upon that house, and could not shake it: for it was founded upon a rock (Luke 6:46-48).

Whether we understand it or not and whether we like it or not, it is undeniably clear that we can count on God's blessings, protection, and provision if we obey Him.

He taught that when we obey Him and do what His Word tells us to do, our homes and families would withstand anything and everything that comes against them.

It never made mention that we would be exempt from storms, but when they came they would not be able to destroy or even shake a home that is protected and guarded by a life of obedience. That is so powerful. Knowing this promise alone makes this life of holiness worth all the effort.

By this we know that we love the children of God, **when we love God, and keep his commandments.** For this is the love of God, that we keep his commandments: and his commandments are not grievous (I John 5:2,3).

Here it is again, proof that we love God is going to be displayed through our obedience to His commandments. It's not always the easy path to obey God, especially when it goes against your logic. Obedience is always connected with trust, and sometimes we don't realize this.

Throughout the ages men, women and young people have fought the inner battle of decision when it seemed like obeying God was the losing choice. For the record's sake and for the sake of someone reading this who is in this battle right now, I want to remind you of what happened to some who chose the tough decision to obey.

Noah looked so foolish to those around him, but he chose to obey the Lord and because of his obedience his entire family was saved.

Abraham's obedience to walk away from everything that was familiar and safe and to look for a city that was mapped out by God resulted in him becoming the father of the great nation Israel.

Joshua won the battle of Jericho by obeying God's unusual and extremely illogical strategy.

Jehoshaphat relied on the guidance of God's Word to go before the Ammonites with praise and worship. It did not make any military sense as he sent the singers ahead of the army. When they began to sing praises to God, the Lord confused the Ammonites and Moabites, and they killed each other. When Jehoshaphat's army reached the battlefield, there was not one survivor.

Peter obeyed Jesus' command to fish in the heat of the day. He caught more fish than ever before.

Paul obeyed God's voice and took the gospel to the Gentiles, because of that, you and I have the honor of knowing this wonderful Lord.

Loving God and keeping His commandments has always gone hand in hand. You cannot have one without the other, but when you have one *with the other* you will open the windows of heaven upon your life and family.

> But take diligent heed to do the commandment and the law, which Moses the servant of the LORD charged you, **to love the LORD your God, and to walk in all his ways, and to keep his commandments**, and to cleave unto him, and to serve him with all your heart and with all your soul (Joshua 22:5).

> If ye love me, keep my commandments…**He that hath my commandments, and keepeth them, he it is that loveth me:** and he that loveth me shall be loved of my Father, and I will love him, and will manifest myself to him (John 14:15,21).

The saints of the Old Testament knew and understood the powerful covenants that were connected to those who loved God and kept His commandments.

> And said, I beseech thee, O LORD God of heaven, the great and terrible God, that keepeth covenant and mercy for **them that love him and observe his commandments** (Nehemiah 1:5).

> And I prayed unto the LORD my God, and made my confession, and said, O Lord, the great and dreadful God, keeping the covenant and mercy **to them that love him, and to them that keep his commandments** (Daniel 9:4).

God's blessings are not always the obvious ones. While the world is popping anti-depressants and spending millions of dollars visiting psychiatrists and therapists, obedience to God's Word will keep you living in true peace, joy and contentment – even in the midst of a storm. You will be blessed with spiritual growth and maturity, the restoration of spiritual authority, and eternal blessings, and you will be rewarded for your obedience on judgment day (Luke 6:21-23).

Obedience is the outward expression of your love for God.

I think I want to say that again.

Obedience is the outward expression of your love for God.

When you love someone deeply you want to please them as Daniel so well demonstrated.

I love the beautiful story of Daniel. As a young teenage boy Daniel had such a desire to please God. His outward expression of love shone brightly when he refused and bow to peer pressure and cultural pressure.

> But Daniel purposed in his heart not to defile himself with the king's own food and wine, and he made request of the prince of the eunuchs that he might not defile himself (Daniel 1:8).

Someone may look at this and say what's the big deal? How could eating someone's food defile another? Let's look at why they believed eating the king's food would bring defilement:

First, the food they served probably would include meats that were declared unclean by the law of Moses. The godly homes these young, teenage boys were taken from had instilled inside of them the importance of obeying the laws of God.

Second, eating the king's food would be giving recognition to the existence of Babylon's false deities. When a person consumed the food dedicated to these false gods, it sent a direct message to others around that they favored those gods. It was like giving their stamp of approval.

Food that was first dedicated to gods was to ensure to the eaters the favor of those gods. In fact, the main reason for Nebuchadnezzar's ordering that the young men eat this prescribed food was to elicit this recognition of deity. Nebuchadnezzar would have insisted that all food coming from the royal kitchen was to be dedicated to these false gods and Daniel and his friends clearly saw through this trickery and recognized they had a decision to make.

This was not just choosing Taco Bell over Morton's Steak House, but this meant punishment and could spoil all chances of advancement toward a position in the king's courts. King's in that day were known for their severe punishments as we see the fiery furnace in this example. Daniel and his three friends probably cringed at the thought of what this decision could mean for them! Not to mention the delicious, quality food that was laid out before them everyday. They watched the other young Jewish boys devour the king's steak and mashed potatoes, and watched how the favor of the king was extended to them while Daniel seemed overlooked in the face of his sacrifice.

I'm sure there were times he wondered if God really saw the sacrifice he was making when he turned and stared into to his plate of vegetables and water. Plus, these guys were a long way from home, away from parents, Rabi's, and miles away from Jewish culture. Nobody would ever know, parents and relatives would never have to find out if they decided to go ahead and join the crowd. It would have been a very natural thing to argue that, since God had not protected them from this captivity, they did not have to be careful in obeying His commands.

So many Christians fall into this category when they feel God has not been "fair" to them, thinking since God let them down they do not have to follow His directions or abide by His ways. If these young men had ever allowed bitterness to overtake them due to the fact they were stripped from their homes and families, they would have never been able to make the strong decisions they did. This shows us Daniel was not ashamed of his faith!

The day he requested to be relieved of the king's order to eat the royal food, even though it did not make a stitch of sense, I'm sure it made a huge impact on Ashpenaz, the prince of the eunuchs. Even if Ashpenaz wasn't especially impressed with the reasoning of Daniel, he must have been impressed by his devotion and love for the God he served. *That he might not defile himself.* Wow, that stirs me.

Now I want you to look at God here.

> **Then God** made Daniel to find kindness and favor before the prince of the eunuchs (Daniel 1:9).

Then God. This brings tears to my eyes when I read this. Daniel's life portrays to you and me what God will do for the person who is faithful in obedience to His will. Daniel determined in his heart to do what was right in God's eyes when it would have been so easy to excuse and do opposite: now we see God stepping on the scene to intervene and help.

Friend of mine, every time you make a decision to do right, every sacrifice you make, every decision you choose that's not easy, God sees it! He keeps good records! He rewards those who are faithful to Him! The story goes on to tell us that God made Daniel to find kindness and favor. If Daniel and his friends had not made the decision to follow the desire and commandments of God, they would not have tasted of this favor.

God's nature and character is the same today as it was years ago when Daniel experienced this. Daniel's relationship with God is what birthed this type of faith, trust, and commitment that gave him the strength to make these decisions. Our consistent prayer life is what provides the fuel to help us stand strong when our flesh is weak.

I want to share Angela's testimony with you:

When I begin to think of all the things God has done for me I can always trace it back to my submission. I was blessed with long, beautiful, thick hair. There was a time in my life when I could have never said that about myself. I used to have such a hatred for my hair. I was embarrassed by how long and thick it was and all I wanted to do was chop it off but instead I just kept it hidden.

I would get headaches from the weight of it and would look for any excuse to justify my desire to cut it. I even tried going to the doctor hoping he would confirm what I was feeling and prescribe that it needed to be cut. My hair just seemed like a burden, as everyday things were more difficult for me. All of this trouble because of my "blessing" that I didn't understand.

Until one day my uncle had a severe stroke and was hospitalized. My family went to visit him and as we were standing in the hospital room my dad looked at me and said, "Angela, put your hair on him and pray." So I did. As I laid my uncut hair over the body of my dying uncle I began to feel the presence of God like I never had before.

To this day I still do not have the proper words to explain what I felt that day. After a few minutes I had finished praying and as I looked around the room there was not a dry eye in that entire area. That was the moment I realized I had hold of something special. You see, I could do something that nobody else in my family could do. Not because I was special or in some way more spiritual than they were, but simply *because I obeyed.* It is not always easy but it is worth it.

A few years later I met the man of my dreams who is now my husband. The first thing he noticed about me was my hair. Little did I know that from the moment he got saved he prayed for a girl with hair to her ankles! I was his answer to prayer! If I would have allowed the way I felt about my hair to determine my actions I don't know where I would be today. All I know is that God's hand is involved in my life like never before, simply because I submitted to what He requires.

The Scriptures plainly reveal that God will instill favor upon those who obey Him. When we seek Him first and not try to figure things out with our own reasoning, He will fulfill every area of our lives including a godly spouse!

Proverbs 16:7 says:
> When a man's ways please the Lord, he maketh even
> his enemies to be at peace with him.

Pleasing God through the methods of love and obedience bring great blessings upon a person's household and personal life. Sometimes the pull of our flesh is too much and we struggle in our attempts to do the right things. Philippians 2:13 tells us we don't have to depend upon our own will, but God will work inside of us as His Spirit *helps us* do the things that please Him.

For it is God which **worketh in you** both to will and
to do of his good pleasure (Philippians 2:13).

Holiness is connected to your relationship with God. There is no
other explanation. When a person quits praying or gets to the place
where the demands and weights of a busy schedule snuff out their
daily prayer and time alone with God, their relationship will suffer.

It may shock you to know that there is a conditional statement in the
New Testament. Many 'Christians' are calling God their father but
not following the directions He requires for this to happen. They pile
a big serving of II Corinthians 6:16,18 on their plate:

I will dwell in them, and walk in them; and I will be
their God, and they shall be my people.
(verse18) And will be a Father unto you, and ye shall
be my sons and daughters, saith the Lord Almighty.

They love the thought of God becoming their Father in these verses,
but never understand that this is a conditional statement made by
God. Right in the middle of this precious promise lays a requirement
in verse 17:

Wherefore come out from among them (the world),
and **be ye separate**, saith the Lord, and touch not the
unclean thing; and I will receive you.

Then … He states:
And will be a Father unto you, and ye shall be my
sons and daughters, saith the Lord Almighty.

He said if you don't touch the things that are unclean, then I will embrace you as my child. What a wonderful trade-off!

What in this world is worth more than God becoming your Father? When life becomes heavy and schedules demanding, when you're feeling all alone in a world where it seems no one understands, when you're broken and bruised, hurt and disappointed, when you just need someone to be there for you ... Jesus will be there.

Going to church is not enough. Singing in the choir, being involved in bible study, teaching Sunday school, all these things are important but they can never replace or substitute a person spending time alone with God each day.

I have learned the devil is really not my greatest enemy - my greatest enemy is my flesh. Believe me, our flesh will fight the desire to pray to the bitter end and the demands of life will provide many excuses of *why* there just is not time to be alone with God each day.

I have battled these seasons in my own busy life and I know first hand the effects this missing ingredient will have upon you. You begin to think differently; you start to justify things you never would have even questioned before. Temptations have a greater pull on you and the tenderness and sensitivity that a prayer life produces is not there to guard your heart.

Friend can I ask, how is your prayer life? I've had to re-evaluate this very question in my own life several times and get my flesh back on track. This means waking up at 5:00am every morning so I can meet with Jesus before anything else in my day starts demanding and pulling at me. I know what a difference this makes in my life and I've learned my flesh is way too strong to try to live this committed lifestyle without a daily searching of my heart and surrendering to God's will. I cannot afford *not* to pray.

There is so much power generated in a daily prayer life! I will go as far as to say this: I don't even know if we can ever really love Jesus the way He has designed us to love Him *without* a consistent prayer life.

The Apostle Paul tried to communicate this secret to God's people when he imparted this in Philippians 2:13. When GOD is inside of you, filling you up with His Spirit daily, it stirs up within you the desire and hunger to do the things that are pleasing to Him. When we are void or low on the oil of relationship, we cannot generate these desires on our own because they war and fight against the desires of our flesh. It sure makes me feel better to know that even Paul wrestled with fighting his flesh when he mentioned in I Corinthians 15:31 that he *died daily.*

This is why relationship with God goes hand in hand with holiness. You cannot separate the two and you cannot have one without the other. When you have a relationship with God you will embrace, seek to understand, and covet the beauty and power of holiness because **God is holy.** As the Scriptures explain, God will work IN YOU, giving you desire and understanding that comes only through those times of sitting at the feet of Jesus.

> As obedient children, not fashioning yourselves according to the former lusts in your ignorance: But as he which hath called you is holy, so be ye holy in

all manner of conversation; Because it is written, Be ye holy; for I am holy (I Peter 1:14-16).

I was sitting in my car in front of the Hampton Inn, talking with a dear friend who had flown in from another state for a conference, as we were just talking about "life."

I had just turned forty a couple of months before this, and as we were talking, suddenly she turned to me and said, "Kim, you're going to face some very unfamiliar and different emotions in this new season of your life. You will fight insecurities that you've never had issues with before, and fears that you have never wrestled with will come at you and attack your mind and emotions. You're going to face some new emotional and mental battles, and I just want to warn you of this."

I listened. I thanked her and thought secretly to myself, "Well, bless her heart, she probably went through some tough times around that age and she's trying to help me, but that won't be me. That's just not my nature."

Within a few months of that conversation which I had totally forgotten about, I was thrown into a whirlwind of fears and insecurities that came out of nowhere. Things I had never battled with before, fears that were very unfamiliar began to enter the corridors of my heart through the doorway of my mind. They began to consume me and affect my thinking.

Nobody but the thief knew I was going through this.

A few months later, my husband and I had saved up to go out of town for our anniversary, just the two of us for our "second honeymoon." I was so excited; I carefully planned out all my outfits and went and got a pedicure. I wanted to feel *gorgeous* for that man that I was still so in love with after all these years. I wanted to look so good for him when I stepped off that plane; I mean I wanted his jaw to literally drop out of socket when he saw me, his beautiful bride of 20 years.

We were like two silly teenagers in love…for about two days. Right in the middle of our little "honeymoon," this whole truckload of fears and insecurities and emotional instability began to pour over me and consume me like a raging river out of control.

Now I don't know if being forty brings a whole new suitcase full of insecurities into a woman's life or what, but in the middle of our little 'honeymoon' this whole cargo of *fear* began to rock pile into my mind until I felt myself literally buried under this mountain of "not feeling good enough, beautiful enough, or skinny enough" and the list gets more detailed, but I will spare you.

All these fears and thoughts were like a broken record in my mind everywhere we went. I felt so alone in this unseen but very brutal world.

We would go to a restaurant, and I would begin to compare myself to other worldly women that sat around us. We walked into a department store, and I would wonder if he was comparing me to how the women looked at the makeup counter. I began to think things like, "I could look so gorgeous if I cut my hair or could wear that kind of makeup." In my mind I *just knew* he was thinking the very same things I was thinking about myself. The devil is such a liar.

Now I had absolutely no justification for my feelings. I have an incredible husband who loves and cares for me; we had twenty years of a fabulous marriage and five kids under our belts. What I'm getting at is this: there was nothing that should have sparked these feelings and thoughts I was having about myself, but they were very real. Never underestimate the power of your mind. Your mind has the power to take flat out lies and make them feel like absolute reality. I was under direct attack and didn't even realize what was happening.

This is exactly where the thief comes on the scene.

He blinds us to the reality of the true beauty of holiness and strives to conform us to the world's standards. Please hear me, the method he uses is F.E.A.R. Fear of not being accepted, fear of not being good enough or pretty enough, fear of never finding a boyfriend or getting married, fear that your friends will reject you. Whatever season of life you are in the thief will use the methods that apply.

The thief watched as I wrestled internally in my secret world of insecurity and fear.

We walked into a department store during our little trip and my husband headed over to the men's department to look at shirts. After about an hour, I had finished so I went to look for him. After combing the entire section of the men's department, I spotted him. He was over on the side looking at a sale rack.

As I approached closer, I could tell he was casually talking with a salesgirl. That was it. Everything I was feeling was right. He didn't love me anymore. My heart began to pound deep inside of my chest, and I could feel fire and smoke coming out my eyeballs, but I knew I couldn't show it.

Now I want to clarify something right here. We're talking Pastor Haney. The most Christian and godly man I know. This man walks in the spirit of integrity and honor. He has never given me a reason to doubt him or to question his integrity. I mean this guy doesn't even look twice at a female bird flying by as he is the safest and most boundary-oriented man I know. Deep inside I knew this. Deep inside I knew what I was feeling was *so wrong*, but the imaginations of my mind that I had been entertaining made an imaginary world seem like reality.

I stormed off, brushing tears from my eyes, and ran up the escalator as I went and hid in the back of the little kids department (how fitting). I did NOT want him to find me. Luckily for me, there was not another soul up there as these tortuous thoughts began to bombard my mind.

What was I going to do? He doesn't love me anymore. I'm not good enough or pretty enough for him anymore. There was a literal battle going on inside this unseen but very real fight that was taking place in my mind. One side was screaming, "You're an idiot. You know everything you're thinking about is wrong. Grow up and get yourself downstairs." The other side was feeding my insecurities that I was already feeling in myself. It's hard to admit, but I almost wanted to believe this.

After about an hour I went downstairs and there he was, waiting in the car. I had my bullets ready and my trigger cocked. I had my script all memorized. I knew exactly what I was going to say. Okay, I know you have never done anything like this…me neither.

I said some things that I knew had hit below the belt. Have you ever said something and right afterwards you feel it weighing inside your chest like you swallowed a tree trunk? You wish you could suck the words back in?

After driving around for about an hour and spilling all these feelings of insecurity I was feeling, I looked at my precious husband, as it all spilled out, "Sometimes I look at these women in the world that are made up to look beautiful, and I think about how beautiful I could look. I see all the fabulous jewelry, the hair designs, the makeup, and the clothes, and it's not always easy saying no. Sometimes it's hard wearing skirts all the time and having long hair that you're trying to style in a classy way and I'm really struggling right now."

As the tears began to roll down my cheeks, and my heart began to be poured out to a man that really didn't know what to do with it all. He just listened. I had never talked to him in this way. I honestly had not remembered ever feeling this way. I was actually even shocking myself by the honesty and the openness I was willing to release. All these lies that I had allowed myself to feed on were pouring out of my heart through my words, but as I look back now I see the footprints and smell the nasty body odor of the thief. Satan singles in on the attack when we are weak or afraid of losing something. He always goes for the jugular vein, the source of where our power is being supplied, which is always our holiness.

Once I finished, he looked at me and quietly asked me, "Kim, do you really believe this message of holiness and separation?" At this point it's just he and I sitting in the car in the parking lot of an outlet mall. It's funny; I had asked myself that same question a few days before. It's like I had a re-evaluation of my life at forty years old. It was time for an exam that wasn't exactly expected nor prepared for.

Why was I the person that I was? Why *did I choose* to dress the way I did? Was it because I was the pastor's wife? Was it because I didn't want to break tradition? Was it because I didn't want to hurt my family? All these questions that I would have never even entertained before were shot into the corridors of my mind and mixed with these emotions and feelings of insecurity. I had to sort through all that mess and come up with a brutally honest answer – not just for him, but also for myself.

The car was just silent for a while as we sat there. (I was actually choking back tears, but I sure didn't want him to know that.) Finally I turned to look at him sitting in the driver's seat and with all the honesty in my heart, I said, "I love you with all my heart, but I don't live this way for you. I don't live this way because I'm the pastor's wife. I don't even live this life of separation because I don't want to bring reproach to the ministry. I couldn't do it; I couldn't pay the price for any of those reasons."

I looked at my husband, with uncontrollable tears now spilling down my face, and said, "I live this because I truly love Jesus." With every corner of my heart searched, the only valid reason I could reply with was because I loved Him. The anchor of my sincere love for Jesus that I built years ago was *holding*.

I had added it all up and that was it. It was as if after all these years, I had to be reminded in myself of WHY I chose this road that was not always an easy one to travel. I thought about my teenage years when the world pulled at me and I had my struggles. This same anchor would always bring me home when others chose a different road. Now here I was, twenty years later, and that same anchor was still holding.

What really makes it worth the cost? It's the only way I can truly give my whole entire life back to this precious Jesus who had been my faithful friend and loving Father throughout my life. This Jesus Who had been there to heal my wounds and take my insecurities and mend my broken heart. Giving Him my life is the only way and the greatest way that I could ever love Him back. As a song that I love, written by Reverend Stan Davidson, reveals, "A lifetime is all I have to give You. It's the only way I have to say I love You."

This may sound strange, but there was a peace that settled on us in that little car that day. Both of us had tears in our eyes because I know that's how my husband feels too. As I made my declaration and had no reason to be dishonest about it, I felt Jesus wrap His loving arms around me that day in the little rental car. I felt His heartbeat that day. Just to hear once again that one of His children serves Him just because she loves Him.

I don't want to go through anymore of those attacks anytime soon, but I felt like a reinforcement of steel was placed into my soul that afternoon. What the devil meant for evil, God meant it for good. I was reminded again how blessed and honored I am to be able to serve the Lord in the beauty of holiness.

I have opened my heart and shared with you what the foundation of this whole Christian walk is all about. Sometimes we are thrown an unexpected life re-evaluation test. It's a test that you cannot prepare for because you never know when it will be given. It comes to all of us and during this time in your life you must base your commitments and decisions on the Word of God. It's the only thing that will stand strong and secure in this crumbling society and flaky religious world in which you and I live.

God has called His church to be different from anything else in this world. We are a "peculiar" people. God's true church walks according to the Word of God and it really does not make any difference what the world thinks. We will never receive their approval, nor do we desire it. I want to challenge you to walk through this world with your head held high, not with pride, but with *godly dignity and honor* in Whom you serve and represent. We have possession of the pearl of great price, worth much more than this world could ever afford to offer!

My friend, you have to keep your eyes on the goal. This world is only a dressing room for eternity, and we are not going to be in this dressing room much longer. Those who have been born again and have walked a committed lifestyle down here on this earth will be taken off this planet when Jesus calls His bride home. Any day now the trumpet is going to sound and we which are alive and remain will be caught up together to meet Him in the air. As hard as it may be, we cannot live for the moment. We have to be watching and waiting for our Lord's return and the thief knows his time is short. Until Jesus comes I want to live under the anointing, power, authority, and the blessings of those who walk in the spirit and liberty of holiness!

And I heard as it were the voice of a great multitude, and as the voice of many waters, and as the voice of mighty thunderings, saying, Alleluia: for the Lord God omnipotent reigneth.

Let us be glad and rejoice, and give honour to him: for the marriage of the Lamb is come, and his wife hath made herself ready.

And to her was granted that she should be arrayed in fine linen, clean and white: for the fine linen is the righteousness of saints.

And he saith unto me, Write, Blessed are they which are called unto the marriage supper of the Lamb. And he saith unto me, These are the true sayings of God.

(Revelation 19:6-9)

Other books by Kim Haney:

Seeds of Jochebed
A daily devotional for mothers to teach their children before going to school each morning. Planting seeds of truth daily.

Christians and Strongholds
Uncovering the secret of spiritual strongholds and the effect they have upon Christians. Learning how to break free and stay free from internal bondage.

God Has a Waiting Room
How to respond when God speaks a promise and then ushers you into His waiting room. A book on faith that teaches us how to react to an unseen world through the works of faith.

Order on amazon.com or CLMinistry.com

Bulk order Information:
Christian Life Center
9025 N. West Lane
Stockton, CA 95210
Kimhaney7@yahoo.com

209.957.4027